Sports Fans Who Made Headlines

Rich Wolfe
&
Dale Ratermann

MASTERS PRESS

A Division of Howard W. Sams & Co.

Published by Masters Press
A Division of Howard W. Sams & Company
2647 Waterfront Pkwy E. Dr, Suite 100
Indianapolis, IN 46214

97 98 99 00 01 02   10 9 8 7 6 5 4 3 2 1

Library of Congress Cataloging-in-Publication Data

Wolfe, Rich.
    Sports fans who made headlines / Rich Wolfe & Dale
Ratermann.
        p. cm.
    ISBN 1-57028-117-3
    1. Sports spectators. I. Ratermann, Dale, 1956- . II. Title.
GV715.W65   1997   97-16786
796--dc21   CIP

ACKNOWLEDGMENTS

The authors would like to thank the many people who contributed to this wonderful collection of stories. Among the most helpful were Brian Brosi, Pete Cava and Dan O'Brien. Others who contributed information were Peter Bjarkman, Jeffrey Boggs, Mark Boyle, Richard Bresciani, John Counsell, Lou D'Ermilio, Alan Fredman, Steve Frost, Cappy Gagnon, Tom Hathaway, Bob Lovell, Bill Mattingly, Tom McGivern, Gary Miller, John Nordahl, Terry Shepard, Tom Shrader, Sam Smith and Jon Spoelstra.

Several good ideas came from requests on news groups on the Internet. Among those who responded were: James Campbell, Bryan Canterbury, David Farrell, Jamie Ford, Ford Lytle Gilmore, Kevin Gross, R. Hernandez, Ed Jones, Jeff Metcalf, D.C. Robinson, Amy Schneider, Robert Souza, Mike Stevens, Robert Stevenson, David C. Valenzuela and Thomas White.

Other background information was obtained from articles in *The New York Times*, *The Los Angeles Times*, *USA Today*, *Sports Illustrated*, the fine series of *Hall of Shame* books (Collier Books) by Bruce Nash and Allan Zullo, and the excellent *Field of Screams* (W.W. Norton & Company) by Richard Scheinin.

Thanks to Tom Bast, Holly Kondras and Heather Lowhorn from Masters Press. And thanks to Chad Wollums, also from Masters Press, for his hard work finding the many fine photographs.

Dedication

For Mom, who will be my biggest fan forever.
                                                    — D.R.

*For three great kids: Duke, Tucker and Thad. And Special K,
the woman with magic.*
                                                    — R.W.

Contents

Football 47

Gridiron Fandemonium: It's A Ball

Hockey 75

Would Be More Fun With A Transparent Puck

Soccer 83

A Game Desperately In Need Of A Shot Clock

Promotions

More Fun Than Eating Watermelon In A Rental Car

Celebrities

So How Come They Get Such Good Seats For Free?

Bits and Bites

Begged, Borrowed and Stolen

INTRODUCTION

Fans. Can't live with 'em. Can't live without 'em.

That's the predicament sports organizations face in today's modern society. But *Sports Fans Who Made Headlines* is not an essay to figure out what makes sports fans tick. Instead, it's a celebration of fans who did the extraordinary and wound up getting attention for it.

It's about fans who went to the ball park for no reason other than to enjoy a game. It's about fans who have a passion for an athlete, a team or a sport. And it's about fans who crossed the line from the stands to center stage on the field of play.

More importantly, it's to show you — a fellow sports fan — that it could be you. Yes, if only you go to the game. You can be the fan catching Eddie Murray's 500th career home run. Yes, you can be the fan chosen at random to make a $1 million shot. Yes, you can be the fan "discovered" on a stadium video screen.

But wait. You don't even have to go to the game. You can be the fan who wins a 1910 Honus Wagner baseball card. Yes, you can be the fan who goes all the way on *The $64,000 Question*. Yes, you can be the fan who makes a living marketing a team's novelty item.

On the darker side, you also can be the fan killed by a flying wheel, a collapsed grandstand or lightning.

Yogi Berra might have said, "Every fan can have 15 minutes of fame, even if the highlight runs on *Sportscenter* for months." So, sit back, get a bag of peanuts, enjoy these moments of fame and realize: *It really could be you*.

The Really Big Fans

The Kid

Twelve-year-old Jeff Maier didn't know when he went to a New York Yankees 1996 playoff game that his life soon would change forever.

Maier stuck out his gloved left hand from the front row of the Yankee Stadium right field stands and deflected Derek Jeter's fly ball into the seats for a game-tying, eighth-inning home run. The Yankees went on to beat the Baltimore Orioles, 5-4, in 11 innings. Maier went on to instant stardom.

The next day he was on *Good Morning America*, *Live with Regis & Kathie Lee* and *Hard Copy*. He turned down a chance to appear on the *Late Show With David Letterman*, *The Larry King Show* and *Geraldo*. He lunched at Manhattan's All-Star Cafe before talking a limo to see the next playoff game from front row seats behind the Yankees' dugout. He signed autographs while reporters stumbled over each other to get a story.

Television replays show that umpire Rich Garcia erred in calling the play a home run. "I thought it was out of the ballpark," said Garcia. "(Maier) reached out. He did not reach down. In my judgment, he did not interfere with the fielder attempting to catch the ball. It probably was a situation where the ball would have hit the wall." Garcia said he would have ruled the play a double if he had the luxury of instant replay.

The play caused a national uproar. Maryland Gov. Parris Glendening half-jokingly said, "I am strongly urging that minor theft charges by brought against the 12-year-old boy who clearly stole the baseball in mid-air."

Maier, from Old Tappan, N.J., tried to silence his critics. "They don't understand. If they were me, a 12-year-old kid at a New York Yankees playoff game, they would try and catch the ball, too."

 That wasn't the first time a fan in Yankee Stadium might have changed the outcome of a game.

- In the first round of the 1996 American League playoffs, Juan Gonzalez of the Texas Rangers hit a drive down the left-field line. Dean Benasillo, a 28-year-old contractor from Brooklyn, sitting on the foul side of the foul pole, reached into fair territory and caught the ball. "The last thing I wanted to do was hurt the team," he said. "I was hoping it was foul. I thought it was foul. I just saw the ball coming at me, and it was my instinct to catch it." It was ruled a home run, despite protests from the Yankees.
- In the heat of the 1993 pennant race, the Boston Red Sox were ahead of the Yankees, 3-1, with two outs in the bottom of the ninth. As Sox pitcher Greg Harris delivered a pitch to Mike Stanley, third base umpire Tim Welke spotted someone running onto the field. Welke called time out, but Harris didn't hear him. Stanley hit a routine fly to left, apparently ending the game. But Welke said he called time before the pitch was made. Given a second chance, the Yankees rallied and won the game, 4-3. The fan later was identified as a 15-year-old boy watching the game with a church group. "We were all trying to get the kid back here to thank him," said Stanley.
- St. Louis Cardinals fan Paul Muehling got a public apology from TV announcer Vin Scully after Muehling was incorrectly accused by Scully of interfering with a ground-rule double. The play cost the San Francisco Giants a run during a 1987 National League playoff game.

Rockin' Rollen, John 3:16

No fan in the history of sports has been more recognizable than Rollen Stewart.

Anyone who watched a nationally televised sporting event in the '70s and '80s can recall his multi-colored Afro wig and John 3:16 sign. But Stewart, a.k.a. Rainbow Man, says he despises sports. "People who go to sporting events are like the Romans who went to watch the lions eat Christians."

He got his inspiration during a visit to Mardi Gras in 1976. "I wanted to get into show business, and I got this vision for a character who could be a people pleaser. I desperately wanted to be noticed and admired. My ultimate goal was to be in the Screen Actors Guild, spend an occasional day shooting a commercial, then sit back and collect the residual checks."

In 1980 Stewart sold his ranch, threw away his wig and switched to the life of an evangelist. But things began to unravel. At the 1991 Masters Tournament, he blew an air horn at the sixteenth green. At Robert Schuller's Crystal Cathedral, he set off stink bombs. He also was suspected of igniting a similar device at the Evander Holyfield-George Foreman title fight. And finally in 1992, he barricaded himself in a Hyatt Regency Hotel at the Los Angeles International Airport. Armed with a .45-caliber automatic weapon, he threatened to shoot at incoming planes if he wasn't given three hours of network television prime time to offer his views of world politics, the weather situation and the Second Coming of Jesus.

A SWAT team broke down the door and arrested Stewart without incident. He was sentenced to three concurrent life sentences and currently resides in a cell in the California prison system.

What's the worst thing about prison? "The loss of my freedom. I was in a position where I had an audience of 2.8 billion through satellite dishes. Now I can only spread my faith in the yard to criminals who consider me a woman."

By the way, what exactly does John 3:16 say? The Gospel of St. John, Chapter 3, Verse 16: "For God so loved the world, that He gave His only begotten Son, that whosoever believeth in Him should not perish, but have everlasting life."

Giles Pellerin is Always There

Giles Pellerin is a University of Southern California football fan. What kind of fan? Well, he's seen a lot of games. Like every one — home and away — since 1926. That's 71 years of cardinal and gold. A total of 774 games with Traveler, the famous white horse mascot. He's seen all eight of USC's national championship teams, all 120 of its first-team All-Americans and all four of its Heisman Trophy winners. He's watched games in 75 different stadiums in more than 50 cities.

Photo courtesy of USC

Not even surgery can keep Giles Pellerin from a USC game.

The 90-year-old former telephone company executive was presented with the Sears DieHard Fan Award in 1996, given to the NCAA Division I "DieHard" sports fan.

Pellerin began his streak as a sophomore student at USC. He watched the Trojans beat Whittier, 74-0, and was hooked. Sure, he's come close to missing a game. In 1993 when he was leaving his hotel after a game at Penn State, he suffered a ruptured aortic abdominal aneurysm. USC had the following weekend off, so after spending 12 days in a Pennsylvania hospital, he ordered his own release and was in the stands for a home game two days later. In 1949 he was hospitalized for an emergency appendectomy. On game day, he told his attendants he was going for a walk on the hospital grounds, but instead high-tailed it to the Coliseum to watch the Trojans. His car's water pump went out near Oklahoma City the day before a game in South Bend, Ind. And in 1969 he ignored his doctor's warnings to stay in bed for six weeks after stomach tumor surgery. After all, USC's opener was only two weeks away.

Pellerin has traveled about 750,000 miles and spent nearly $100,000 to keep his streak intact.

"People ask me why I go all the way across the states to see a game that only lasts two or three hours," said Pellerin. They say, 'Isn't it a waste of time?' Well, it isn't. I get to meet friends in various parts of the country, see campuses. It's more than just a football game. It's the friendships you make along the way.

"Sure, I could sit in my rocking chair and grow old, but I don't intend to do that. You've got to have something to look forward to. I've always said that going to the USC games is the thing that has kept me alive, young and happy!"

 Giles isn't the only Pellerin who supports the Trojans. His younger brother, Oliver, hasn't missed a game since 1945 and is nearing 600 consecutive games; another brother, Max, had a 300-plus game streak snapped when his work took him overseas. Here are some more dedicated fans:

• Roger and Doris Goodridge of Baldwinsville, N.Y., have attended every Colgate football game — home and away — since 1940.

That's 540 straight games.

- Al Ostermann began attending games at Yale in 1914. He missed only one home game after that. It was in 1930. Yale had an easy match-up with Alford College, so Ostermann went to New York to watch undefeated Army play Illinois.
- Ohio State fan Orlas "Neutron Man" King had his streak of seeing every home football game snapped at 27 years after suffering a heart attack at a pep rally in 1996. He got his nickname from his spirited dancing to OSU's marching band performances, especially its rendition of the "Neutron Dance."
- Howard Foering saw 99 consecutive games in the Lehigh-Lafayette football series before he died at age 106 in 1975.

Michael Pantazis Dives into Celebrity

The scene was Chicago's Soldier Field. A 1995 Monday Night Football Game between the Bears and the Green Bay Packers. The Bears' Kevin Butler booted an extra point, and the ball sailed into the tunnel behind the goal post. What ABC's cameras picked up was Michael Pantazis diving out of the stands, his body outstretched, catching the ball securely with both hands, tucking it against his chest, then falling 25 feet on his back onto an usher who never saw what hit him. No one was hurt on the asphalt floor under Gate O, and miraculously, Pantazis held onto the ball.

"I saw the ball coming over the middle and, I'm sorry, but I just had to go for it," said the 28-year-old Chicago roofer. "I almost had one last week, and it hit right off my hand. I couldn't let this one get away."

Rather than eject Pantazis, the security staff at Soldier Field let him keep the ball and return to his seat. Soon he was doing interviews for the local media, as well as a national network. Pantazis parlayed his leap into an appearance on *Late Night With David Letterman*.

His high school football coach, Mike Pols, just happened to be watching the game on TV. "I watched the replay and said, 'Wow! Whoever did that had to be really crazy.' Then I saw the guy being interviewed and said, 'Holy s___, that's Mike!' Within 10 minutes after that interview, I got seven calls. I've never seen anything like this."

Strangely enough, it wasn't the first time a fan jumped out of his seat at Soldier Field to snare an extra point. In the 1970s, 41-year-old Larry Stakenas did a similar leap. "One of my dreams is to get a ball, any kind of ball," he said. He dove over the wall, missed the ball and fell right into a tuba.

The Cameron Crazies

The Chicago Cubs' Bleacher Bums (see page 13) and former Cleveland Browns' Dawg Pound (see page 47) are among the best groups of fans in sports. But the cheering section that ranks No. 1 in fervor, enthusiasm and creativity holds court in Cameron Indoor Stadium at Duke University.

The Cameron Crazies have rocked college basketball games with their signs, chants, distractions and verbal abuses. The student cheering section uses foreign languages. (A sign against North Carolina proclaimed in Latin, *Eruditia et Basketballia*, and when Detlef Schrempf attempted a free throw, the group chanted, *"Fehlwurf!"* which means "air ball."). It uses props. (When Chris Washburn showed up for a game after being arrested for stealing

The Cameron Crazies in action.

a stereo, he was showered with headphones, album covers and records. When Lorenzo Charles was caught stealing pizzas, dozens of pizza boxes littered the floor upon his arrival.) It might also use some tact. (After Maryland's Herman Veal was disciplined for alleged misconduct with a coed, he was bombarded with more than 1,000 women's panties. A sign asked, "Hey Herm, did you send her flowers?")

The Duke mascot even got in a tasteless act. In a game against Notre Dame, the Devil wore a headband marked "Buckwheat" to make fun of David Rivers.

The students occupy 300 seats around the court on a first-come, first-served basis. Lines form the night before a game, and when the doors open two hours before tip-off, the students are primed for action.

Duke coach Mike Krzyzewski is apologetic to opposing teams and officials of the Atlantic Coast Conference, but in reality the fans give him a home-court advantage. Not only do they get opposing players and coaches to lose their train of thought on the court, but their free throw distractions have gone high-tech. Students were chastised for using a pen-light to shoot a low-level laser in the eyes of opposing shooters.

Through it all, the Duke students just want to appreciate good basketball. They repeatedly bowed to Bobby Hurley and chanted, "We're not worthy." When Grant Hill's parents were introduced to the crowd prior to their son's final home game, they were engulfed with the chant, "Another son! Another son!"

One tradition that has caused the school some consternation is the rite of building a bonfire in the main quadrangle to celebrate any Final Four victory. Students have been injured and arrested; University property has been destroyed.

The only time the Crazies were one-upped by the opposition was by Brown forward James Joseph. Every time a visiting player fouls out, the students begin a long, loud "Ooooooooooh" until the player sits down. Then they yell, "See ya!" But when Joseph fouled out with 2:44 remaining in the game, he stood in front of the team bench, rather than sit down. For 13 minutes, the crowd, gasping for air, continued its "Oooooh," but Joseph never did sit down. Finally, with the game over and the teams leaving the court,

8

the students let loose with a less than enthusiastic, "See ya." "He had us scouted," said a Dukie. "I can't believe it."

Morganna, the Kissing Bandit

Morganna Roberts spent the '70s and '80s showing up at sporting events to kiss unsuspecting athletes and coaches. The professional dancer sports impressive statistics: 60-24-39.

She's been arrested for trespassing more times than she can remember, and has never failed to pay a fine. But she has gotten out of a few citations by using the gravity defense: "This woman with a 112-pound body and 15-pound chest leaned over the rail to see a foul ball," said her attorney. "Gravity took its toll, she fell out on the field, and the rest is history."

AP / Wide World Photos

Morganna The Kissing Bandit steals a kiss from Steve Yeager.

Morganna was raised by her grandmother, who sent her off to boarding school in Peewee Valley, Ky. She could tell from an early age that she was blessed with an extra-large bosom. That eventually led to a career in show business and a publicity stunt that obviously keeps working.

The Kissing Bandit broke into the big leagues in 1970 at Cincinnati's Riverfront Stadium. "I was with some friends and I kissed Pete Rose on a double-dirty dare. Who would know that it would snowball into this?"

Since then, her list includes Fred Lynn, Lance Parrish, George Brett, Steve Garvey, Don Mattingly, Steve Yeager, John Candelaria, Nolan Ryan, Cal Ripken, Mike Schmidt, Kareem Abdul-Jabbar, Frank Layden and The Chicken. She began taking the act on the road and teams used it as a promotional tool to increase attendance. She even got a jockey at a race track.

Her favorite "victim" was George Brett. "He's a great kisser and a fantastic baseball player." Jim Palmer ranked second. "He looks so cute in his undies."

Guenter Parche Stabs Monica Seles

It was one of the scariest moments in sports. It was an event that was waiting to happen. German Guenter Parche came out of the stands of a 1993 tennis tournament in Hamburg, Germany, and stabbed Monica Seles, the world's top-ranked female player.

The 19-year-old Yugoslav, sitting courtside between sets, was stabbed between her shoulder blades with a 4 1/2-inch boning knife. The blade went a half-inch deep into the muscles and narrowly missed the spinal cord. As Seles received medical attention, Parche was wrestled to the ground by two security guards.

Parche, who said he didn't want to kill Seles, was upset that fellow German Steffi Graf wasn't ranked No. 1. The 39-year-old unemployed lathe operator was given a two-year suspended sentence by Judge Elke Bosse. After an appeal, Judge Gertraut Goering upheld the sentence, saying Parche had an "abnormal personality structure," but no longer represented a threat to society.

Graf, who had a fan follow her to a practice court in Germany then slashed his wrists in front of her in 1989, said, "I'm not afraid.

Tennis players have more or less been put on a stage. I think we need to be even closer to the people who watch us. You can't live with that fear."

Seles, on the other hand, stayed secluded and received psychological counseling. Her emotional pains lasted long after the knife wound healed. It was 27 months before she returned to competitive tennis.

Baseball

The Bleacher Bums

The Bleacher Bums in Chicago's Wrigley Field claim to be the World's Greatest Baseball Fans. Who can argue? The fans have continued to fill the outfield bleachers despite not winning a World Series since 1908.

What other group of fans had a Broadway play (*Bleacher Bums*) based on it?

And what other group is so powerful that it can all but force its members to throw back home run balls hit by the opposition?

Among the Bums' most noteworthy moments were:

In 1963, the entire front row of fans spent half the game tearing up newspapers and scorecards. Then in the sixth inning as the Dodgers' Frank Howard went back to the warning track to catch a fly ball, the fans hurled their confetti into the air. Howard misplayed the ball, and despite the Dodgers' protests, the play stood.

Fans also concocted the idea that when opposing hitters were at the plate, the fans in the center field seats put on white T-shirts, making it more difficult for the batter to pick up the white ball coming out of the pitcher's hand. Conversely, the same fans switched to black shirts between innings to make it easier for Cub hitters to see the ball. Not amused by the home field advantage, Major League Baseball forced the Cubs to close down the section and a league-wide policy of dark backdrops in center field was adopted.

In 1987, Jerry Pritikin, known as the "Bleacher Preacher," was thrown out for throwing a Frisbee on the field. A regular Bum, Pritikin always wore a shirt that read, "Jerry Pritikin, Bleacher Preacher, The Gospel of the Cubs." The next game, his shirt read, "This Space for Rent."

Another regular Bum is Ronnie Wickers, a.k.a. "Ronnie Woo Woo." He cheers at every game. But his cheers always are the same: "Cubs, Woo! Cubs, Woo! Cubs, Woo!" Over and over again, for the entire game. A self-proclaimed street person, he lives in a Cubs uniform. "When you're a Cub fan, you're halfway to heaven," he said. "You see the blue skies and the white clouds, and there's nothing but Cubs. You don't worry about the strains of life. Wintertime here just ain't the same. It gets lonely. That's why the minute the season ends, I figure out how many hours I need to get to Opening Day. Every morning, I refigure. Just the thought that the Cubs are a day closer helps me get by."

In 1988, on Harry Caray Day, fans received a free plastic beer mug. The Bums threw so many at Reds center fielder Tracy Jones that the game had to be delayed.

Close relatives to the Bleacher Bums are the Cubs fans who sit on the roofs of the buildings across the street from Wrigley Field. The roof at 3649 North Sheffield Avenue comes complete with a bathroom, AstroTurf carpeting, barbecue grill and built-in bleachers. Others are more primitive, but all are filled whenever there is action in Wrigley.

The Cubs chose one fan, 91-year-old Harry Grossman, to turn on the lights at Wrigley Field's first night game Aug. 8, 1988 (8/8/88). He had written a letter to the Cubs earlier in the year to inform them of his life-long passion for the team. "I guess I've seen over 4,000 games in my lifetime," he claimed. Putting that number in perspective, you would have to see every home game for 50 years to reach 4,000. "Baseball and the Cubs have kept me going all these years. I live for the ball games at Wrigley Field. It gives me something to fill my day." His message to other Cubs fans? "Watch the Cubs. Pray for them. We need to win the World Series again. Badly."

Few baseball fans have attended as many games as Grossman, but some have gone to games in every major league park. A few of those spectators stand out:

- Wayne Zumwalt of Colorado Springs attended a Major League game at all 28 Major League stadiums in 28 consecutive days from June 10-July 7, 1993.
- Helen Hudson not only visited every Major League stadium in 1990, she performed the national anthem in each park.
- Bill Craib and Sue Easler of New Hampshire spent the entire summer in 1991 visiting all 178 major and minor league ball parks. Craib, then 27, had worked for a minor league baseball team when he conceived of the idea. He talked Easler, then 23 and a waitress, into going with him in his new Plymouth. The trek began in Oakland and ended in New York. The pair camped out most nights and picked up corporate sponsors and heightened media coverage as the trip continued.

Fans and Streaks

In a recent newspaper article, Justin Rehm of St. Paul, Ind., claims to hold the world record by watching games in 35 Major League ball parks. (Among modern day players, Rusty Staub, Frank Robinson and Eddie Murray hold the record by playing in 32 stadiums.) Rehm, 63, is a retired teacher who has traveled to see such highlights as Stan Musial's final game, Pete Rose breaking Ty Cobb's record for base hits and Cal Ripken's record-breaking consecutive games streak.

But wait. Dr. Seth Hawkins, also of St. Paul (Minnesota, not Indiana) and also a retired teacher, claims in a published account to have attended Major League games in all 54 ball parks used since 1950. He also likes to take in events, like Rose and Ripken's record-setting games, as well as a number of other milestones. But Hawkins' No. 1 claim is seeing the last 13 players record their 3,000th career hit. (That list includes Aaron, Mays, Clemente, Kaline, Rose, Brock, Yastrzemski, Carew, Yount, Brett, Winfield, Murray and Molitor.)

Sports Fans Who Made Headlines

Several other baseball fans have gotten involved in teams' winning or losing streaks:

- A Kansas farmer turned out to be the best good luck charm in history. Charles Faust, a skinny 30-year-old with no previous baseball experience, contacted New York Giants manager John McGraw in 1911 and requested a tryout. Faust had been told by a fortune teller in Wichita that he would become the greatest pitcher in the world if he joined the Giants; he would help the Giants win the pennant; and he would meet a woman named Lulu and sire future generations of baseball stars. Faust, dressed in a dark suit and derby, warmed up. His pitches were so slow, McGraw caught them bare handed. Still, McGraw let Faust sit on the bench for two games. Faust followed the team to its next series, and McGraw again allowed him to sit on the bench. The Giants won, so Faust became a regular in the dugout. The Giants moved into first place, and the entire team credited its good luck charm. Once the Giants clinched the pennant, McGraw actually let Faust pitch in two games, giving up two hits and two runs in two innings. Eventually, Faust left the team and signed a vaudeville contract, but not until he was firmly planted in the baseball history books.

- In Baltimore in 1988, after the Orioles lost their first 10 games, radio disc jockey Mike Filippelli bet his broadcast partner that the losing streak wouldn't get to 13 games. The payoff? Filippelli had to crawl and walk 10,000 meters, which took him four hours. Then attired in an Orioles uniform, he sat in a children's swimming pool in the middle of a shopping mall while he was covered with 30 gallons of chocolate syrup, cherries, pineapple, nuts and whipped cream.

- Diana Deis, an 18-year-old student from Milwaukee, spent 18 hours a day for more than two months on top of a 40-foot tower while she waited for the Milwaukee Brewers to win seven games in a row in 1973. She finally was forced to end her vigil when she caught pneumonia.

Fans as Cheerleaders

Some fans also gained notoriety as team cheerleaders. You know the ones; they're always there, always in the same seat. Sometimes you can count on them more than the players.

- Hilda Chester was the loudest Brooklyn Dodgers fan at Ebbets Field. She began going to games in the '30s. Seated in the center field bleachers, Hilda complemented her booming voice by beating a frying pan. She switched to brass bells, then settled for a cowbell after injuring her wrist in the '40s. Day after day, Hilda was there, ringing the cowbell to encourage the players and fans. She became known throughout the country as the symbol of the Dodgers.

- In Cleveland, John Adams sits high up in the outfield bleachers of Jacobs Field. He buys a second ticket so his bass drum can be at the stadium, too. Adams first took his drum to an Indians game in 1973. He's been beating it at nearly every home game since. A data systems analyst for the local telephone company, Adams says, "People have come up to me for two decades now and said, 'Thank you for being here, because when I'm not at a game, I know you're here for me.'"

- In Baltimore, Wild Bill Hagy gained fame during the 1979 World Series as the fan who spelled out the team's name by moving his body into the shape of letters. Perched on the Orioles' dugout, Hagy led the crowd in the cheers. The cab driver continued his act until 1983 when "it got to a point where it was too demanding," he said. "What I did was just a fun thing. When it quit being fun, I just quit doing it."

- In Anaheim in 1980, Joe Badame, a 35-year-old roofer and magician, attempted to be the California Angels' self-anointed mascot. First, he tried a homemade halo made out of a coat hanger and aluminum foil. The halo by itself wasn't enough, so he donned a gorilla suit, too. He led cheers and bounded around the stadium to the delight of the fans. But when his suit began to smell, and the Angels fell into a dismal losing streak, the fans — and team management — didn't want the gorilla around any more. Said Badame after learning of his expulsion, "Why are they blaming me? I'm not on their pitching staff."

Hecklers

Every sport has its hecklers. Baseball is certainly no exception. Among the most memorable baseball hecklers:

- Pete Adelis, known as "The Leather Lung of Shibe Park," could be heard at Philadelphia A's games from 1940-55. Adelis collected gossip about opposing players' private lives and let everyone in the ball park hear about them.

- In St. Louis, Mary "The Horse Lady" Ott entertained the Browns' and Cardinals' fans in Sportsman's Park from 1926-55. Possessing a screeching laugh that resembled a horse's whinny, Mary didn't need cheers or yells. She just laughed the umpires and opposition into frustration.

- In Philadelphia in 1926, Athletics manager Connie Mack had fan Harry Donnelly arrested for heckling the A's in Shibe Park. Donnelly was fined $500 for disturbing the peace.

- Mack wasn't as successful at quieting the Kessler Brothers. In 1932, the pair sat on opposite sides of the field and heckled the hometown Athletics. Among their targets was third baseman Jimmy Dykes. The Kesslers — Eddie and Bull — abused Dykes so much that he could no longer field a ground ball or get his bat on the ball. Mack tried taking the brothers to court, but the case was thrown out. Mack had only one other option. He sold Dykes to the Chicago White Sox.

- In Brooklyn's Ebbets Field in the '20s, "Abie the Iceman" became known for the jeering he rained on the Dodgers from the upper deck. Fed up with the heckling of the hometown team, Dodger management offered Abie a free season's pass if he only stopped his yelling. Abie agreed, but a few days later he showed up at the front office and turned in his pass. The enjoyment went out of watching the games if he couldn't ridicule the players. Abie returned to paying his own way into the upper deck, and the heckling resumed.

- At the turn of the century, an umpire was arrested and fined for heckling the crowd. In Spartanburg, S.C., umpire William Henderson made a call that displeased the hometown fans. The umpire was struck with a bottle and bombarded with verbal abuse. He turned to the stands, shouted loudly and brandished a "knife" in his hand. The ump was escorted off the field and taken to the jail. He was charged with using profane language and threatening the patrons. Henderson denied the charges, but was fined $15.

 Hecklers sometimes rile the players so much that the players try to get even:

• California Angels designated hitter Chili Davis claimed he was taunted while he stood in the on-deck circle at Milwaukee's County Stadium. Davis walked over to the first row of box seats and said to Andy Johannsen, "You got a problem with me, say it to my face." Davis then poked and slapped the 26-year-old fan. Davis was fined $287 by the county and another $5,000 by the American League.

• Also in Milwaukee, Chicago White Sox outfielder Tony Phillips punched a fan in the face after hearing what he claimed were racial slurs. The incident happened after Phillips was removed from a game in the seventh inning. Phillips changed into street clothes, then motioned to fan Chris Hovorka to meet him under the stands. According to Hovorka, "He gets in my face and says, 'You're talking a lot for a fat white boy.' I said, 'You should be used to heckling.' He clobbered me twice, I hit the ground, and he left." Phillips (and Hovorka) were fined $287 by the county. Phillips also received a $5,000 fine from the American League.

• Albert Belle has had run-in after run-in with fans. Among Belle's transgressions are: chasing a fan in the stands while still in college, throwing a baseball at a fan, throwing a baseball at a photographer, insulting a fan in Texas who wanted to trade a home run ball for an autograph, cursing an NBC reporter at the World Series, chasing teenagers who threw eggs at his house on Halloween, threatening a reporter who was standing behind the batting cage before a game and throwing a cup of Gatorade at a cameraman. A family reportedly drove hundreds of miles to the Indians' spring training camp, found Belle on the field and told him they'd come all that way just for an autograph. Belle replied, "Guess you came all that way for nothing." His relations with fans got so bad that Belle released a statement praising his hometown fans in Cleveland in 1996: "The All-Star Break gives me a chance to tell you all how much I appreciate your support over the last few years, and this one in particular...The positive reception I receive from you each time we play in Cleveland has been a great comfort to me. I know I can count on a warm homecoming from all of you whenever the team walks onto Jacobs Field. That knowledge has sustained me; it has been a major force in my effort to do my best for the Indians, and for all of you."

- Cincinnati pitcher Rob Dibble was suspended four days and fined an undisclosed amount for throwing a ball into the stands and hitting Meg Porter, a first grade teacher, on the elbow.

 The good ole days? Players knew how to rough up fans in the old days, too...

- Ty Cobb was known for going after any fan that looked cross-eyed at him. He even beat up a man who was missing one hand and three fingers off the other hand. When told that he was picking on an invalid, Cobb supposedly replied, "I don't care if he has no feet!" Rube Waddell went into the stands to challenge fans as often as he went to the pitcher's mound.
- Billy Martin was known for getting into lots of fights both on and off the field. As a player for the Yankees, he was involved in a 1957 brawl at the Copacabana in New York that included five star players. Martin soon was traded to Kansas City. As the Yankees manager, Martin's most publicized fight with a fan was in 1979 when he punched marshmallow salesman Joe Cooper.
- Babe Ruth also had a few run-ins with fans, but he's best remembered by his act of kindness toward Johnny Sylvester. The 11-year-old was badly injured in a fall from a horse prior to the 1926 World Series. To cheer him up, Sylvester was presented with autographed balls from the Yankees and Cardinals, along with a promise from Ruth to hit a home run for the boy.

Ruth hit four home runs in the Series, and Sylvester made a miraculous recovery.

Sometimes hecklers can leave their marks on overly sensitive players:

- Tonya Moore, widow of former California Angels pitcher Donnie Moore, claimed in 1990 that the fans who continually jeered her husband contributed to the frustration that eventually induced him to kill himself. "I'll never forgive the fans for what they did to my husband. Never, ever."
- New York Yankees pitcher Ed Whitson felt so much pressure from the hometown fans that he pitched only away games during the second half of the 1985 season.
- In 1943 in Detroit, Tigers star Rudy York was driven to the verge of a nervous breakdown from hecklers. York helped lead the Tigers to the 1940 World Series with 33 home runs and 134 RBI, but when he slumped in 1943, the hometown fans booed him incessantly. Finally, local sportswriters appealed to the fans to lighten up. The fans cooled it, and York responded with 17 homers and 42 RBI — in one month.

Who Says There's No Action?

Chicago Cubs pitcher Randy Myers was attacked on the mound by a fan in Wrigley Field in 1995. After pinch-hitter James Mouton hit a home run off Myers, John Murray jumped from the stands and ran toward Myers. The hurler, trained in martial arts, dropped the fan with a forearm, and the two wrestled on the ground before other players and security personnel pulled the fan away. Murray, a 27-year-old bond trader at the Chicago Board of Trade, was banned from Cubs home games for a year, given 18 months probation, a $500 fine and ordered to volunteer 200 hours of community service.

- Murray wasn't the first fan to challenge a player on the field. In 1952, after St. Louis Browns pitcher Earl Harrist hit two Red Sox in a game at Boston, a one-legged Sox fan hobbled out to the mound on crutches and scolded Harrist.

- In Chicago's Comiskey Park in 1960, Willie Harris was about to lose a bet, because of an error committed by White Sox infielder Sammy Esposito. Harris jumped onto the field and went after Esposito. Security guards swarmed on Harris just as he got to Esposito and swung wildly at the second baseman.
- Frank Germano became somewhat of a cult hero in 1940 when he jumped out of the stands and attacked an umpire. Following a Brooklyn Dodgers loss in Ebbets Field, Germano, a 21-year-old petty thief, wrestled umpire George Magerkurth to the ground and landed several punches before he was pulled away. At the trial the ump withdrew his charges, releasing the young man. Much later, Germano revealed that he was intentionally creating a disturbance so his partner in crime could pick a few pockets in the stands.
- Frank Kuraczea, Jr., also attacked an umpire. It was Oct. 9, 1981 in Yankee Stadium during an American League playoff game. Third base umpire Mike Reilly called out Yankee Dave Winfield on a close play. At the end of the inning Kuraczea leaped onto the field and jumped on Reilly's back, cursing and swinging his fists. Yankee third baseman Graig Nettles grabbed the fan as police pulled Kuraczea away. He was arrested and charged with illegal possession of a dangerous weapon — he had a blackjack in his pocket — as well as criminal trespassing and disorderly conduct.
- Probably the only time an official scorer was attacked by fans was in 1933. Joe DiMaggio was a minor leaguer in the Pacific Coast League and working on a 61-game hitting streak (years before his record 56-game hitting streak in the Major Leagues). In Game No. 60 on the road at Sacramento, DiMaggio had his streak continue on a questionable call by the official scorer, Steve George. Fans stormed the press box and tried to get at George. The police were called in, and George was escorted from the stadium.
- To celebrate the Fourth of July in 1900, thousands of Chicago Cubs fans fired their guns into the air every time the home team scored. The fans in the covered right field bleachers got so rowdy that they riddled the roof with holes when the Cubs

tied the game in the ninth. After the Cubs won in extra innings, the fans fired every remaining round, sending the visiting Philadelphia players scurrying for cover. Miraculously, no one was injured.

• Fans watching the New York Yankees win the World Series in 1996 got a lot of attention. At one home game, seven young males were cited for running onto the field and fined $50. There also were 122 people arrested for peddling and ticket scalping. One man panhandling outside Yankee Stadium held up a sign: "Hey, why lie, I need a beer." Meanwhile, a street vendor was selling a cartoon poster entitled "Stranger in New York." It featured an Atlanta Braves fan asking a Yankees fan, "Can I ask where the Empire State Building is or should I just go to hell?" During the team's victory parade in Manhattan, two fans rode on their own float, Pee Wee Scheidt, who was first in line for playoff tickets, and Freddy "The Fan" Schuman, a pot-banging regular in the Stadium's upper deck.

• Those same Yankees fans caused an embarrassment for the franchise, as well as the entire country. In a 1983 game vs. the Toronto Blue Jays, the fans booed the Canadian national anthem so loudly that New York Mayor David Dinkins and Yankees owner George Steinbrenner were forced to issue public apologies.

• When the Washington Senators played their final game in the nation's capital in 1971, just 14,460 die-hards attended. But by the eighth inning, it seemed like more when they began climbing out of the stands to shake hands with the players and run around the field. Play was suspended while the diamond was cleared. With two outs in the ninth, the fans swarmed the field again, this time ripping up the turf, the bases, home plate and the pitching rubber. Scoreboard lights were taken as souvenirs, as well as anything that wasn't nailed down.

• Philadelphia fans, doubling as souvenir hunters, nearly dismantled Connie Mack Stadium after the final out in the final game of 1970. Each fan was presented with a seat slat, but those wooden instruments became weapons and tools as rowdy spectators ran onto the field and hacked down signs. One fan even disconnected a toilet and took it home.

- In 1907 fans in the New York Giants' Polo Grounds celebrated a cold Opening Day by throwing baseball-sized snowballs onto the field. The first snowball didn't appear until the eighth inning, but once the fans got the hang of it, they were relentless. Finally, the umpires called off the game and awarded a victory to the visiting Phillies.

- Fans in Boston wanting to see the 1903 World Series stormed the gates and milled around the field. Police were called in, and the fans were squeezed onto the outfield warning track. A ground-rule was added that any ball going into the crowd was a double. Later in the same Series, Pittsburgh fans wanted to help their hometown Pirates, so they dumped baskets of shredded paper into the infield breeze, hoping to distract the Boston hitters.

- At the 1973 National League Playoffs, New York Mets fans were riled when Cincinnati's Pete Rose toppled Mets shortstop Bud Harrelson while breaking up a double play. When Rose returned to his position in the outfield, fans pelted the field with so much garbage that the Reds retreated to the dugout. The Mets sent Willie Mays out to the stands to plead with the fans to stop their littering. It worked, but the fired up Reds beat the Mets, 9-2.

- Pete Rose also incited Cincinnati fans to a near riot in 1988. Instead of being the attention of their ire, Rose's disgust of umpire Dave Pallone caused the fans to bombard the ump with garbage. Finally, after a 15-minute delay, Pallone removed himself from the game.

- In the 1934 World Series, St. Louis Cardinal Joe Medwick got into a fracas with the Detroit Tigers' third baseman in the sixth inning after a hard slide. When Medwick took his position in left field, Detroit fans pelted him with garbage. He retreated to the dugout. Teammate Leo Durocher ordered him back to the outfield. The fans continued their barrage. Again Medwick headed for cover. Three times Medwick tried to resume his position until Commissioner Kenesaw Mountain Landis ordered Cardinals manager Frank Frisch to remove

Medwick from the game. The commissioner may have been influenced by the Cardinals' 9-0 lead.

- In 1894 young fans sitting under the right field bleachers in Boston's South End Baseball Grounds set fire to an abandoned wood pile. Soon the bleachers were engulfed in flames. A stiff breeze spread the embers and before fire fighters could extinguish the blaze, the entire new ball park was destroyed, along with 12 acres of the neighborhood. A total of 182 families were left without homes.

Sometimes fans carry their adoration beyond the field and become obsessed with the players:

- In 1949 Eddie Waitkus was shot by 19-year-old Ruth Ann Steinhagen, a Chicago typist who had constructed a shrine for the player at the foot of her bed. Steinhagen had never spoken to Waitkus, but she became despondent over his trade from the Chicago Cubs to the Philadelphia Phillies. When he returned to Chicago with the Phillies, she was waiting at the Edgewater Beach Hotel, where the team was staying. She left Waitkus a stack of messages to go to her room. He knocked on her door. When she opened it, she told him, "I have a surprise for you." He entered the room. Steinhagen went to the closet, took out a rifle and shot him. She called the front desk and informed the hotel of the shooting. Waitkus recovered and returned to the Phillies' line-up the following season. Steinhagen spent three years in a mental hospital, then disappeared.
- In 1995, Tricia Miller, a 31-year-old factory worker from Port Hope, Ont., became obsessed with Toronto's Roberto Alomar. She claims to have been spurned by the player after a brief sexual encounter. She was arrested carrying a loaded handgun in Toronto's SkyDome Hotel where Alomar lived. Alomar denied having had any relationship with Miller. She was sentenced to nine months in jail.
- In 1996, Larina Lewis allegedly made a Molotov cocktail and said she would toss it at Cincinnati Reds shortstop Barry Larkin. The 26-year-old woman reportedly told neighbors she

had made the weapon and asked for directions to Larkin's home.

Baseball fans have gotten injured at games in a variety of ways:

- Vince Coleman, playing for the New York Mets, threw a lighted firecracker from a vehicle, injuring three autograph seekers — including two-year-old Amanda Santos — outside Dodger Stadium in Los Angeles following a 1993 game. Driving the Jeep was Dodgers outfielder Eric Davis. "Although I had no warning and did not know that a passenger in my car was about to do something that might injure someone, I deeply regret that the incident occurred," Davis said. "As the father of two young children, I know the danger associated with fireworks and I have the utmost concern for anyone who may have been injured." The fans, though, were upset. "I'm angry at them because they thought it was funny," said Cindy Mayhew of Covina, Calif., who also was injured.
- In 1990, nine-year-old Michelle Taft suffered a broken jaw when she was hit by a foul ball while watching the Seattle Mariners. She was smacked by a ball off the bat of Mariners third baseman Darnell Coles.
- Meanwhile, Joann Barrett was shot in the hand while sitting in the upper deck of Yankee Stadium in 1985. The shooter was never found, but police said the shot had to have been fired from inside the Stadium. Asked if she would continue to attend Yankees games, Barrett replied, "I am a Mets fan now."
- An unidentified woman was injured at Cleveland's Jacobs Field in 1996 when peanut vendor Dan Kudroff struck her in the face with an errant toss, dislodging her contact lens, overturning her nachos and forcing her to leave the ball park early. Following the incident, the stadium concessionaire imposed a no-throwing rule.
- One fan's life was saved by the quick action of Texas Ranger Doc Medich. The pitcher had worked as a resident physician in the off-season in hopes of becoming a doctor full-time when he retired. While he was running wind sprints in the outfield

prior to a game in Baltimore in 1978, he rushed into the stands to help Germain Languth of Pasadena, Md. The 61-year-old had suffered a heart attack. Medich administered mouth-to-mouth resuscitation and heart massage for nearly 30 minutes before the fan was transported to a hospital.

Baseball: A Game For Lovers?

- Fans watching the Seattle Mariners play the Blue Jays in Toronto's SkyDome in 1990 got a little extra action for their price of admission. Attached to the stadium is a hotel. Some of the rooms have windows overlooking the field. On that particular day an amorous couple engaged in a sex act in full view of the crowd. To put a stop to such behavior, hotel guests now are required to sign a pledge of conduct not to engage in any activities considered inappropriate in public.

- At a 1995 game in Dodger Stadium, Melvin Hoffman and Regina Chatien were caught in the middle of a sex act while seated in the stands. Hoffman, 53, and Chatien, 43, were spotted by an off-duty police officer who happened to be at the game with his four children. Hoffman and Chatien were ordered by the courts to serve 120 hours of community service and to purchase 100 tickets to future Dodger games for charity. In addition, they were put on two years probation and ordered to stay away from Dodger Stadium during that time.

- But perhaps the most daring act of public sex at a baseball game occurred during the post-game celebration following Bobby Thomson's home run in the 1951 playoffs. Relates spectator Arnold Winick: "I was down on the field, trying to get at one of the players just to touch him. You've never seen such an outpouring of pure hysterical glee. It was like a million people all having a communal orgasm. I saw a man and a woman lying in the dirt along the railing by the first base boxes, right next to the dugout, and he had his fly open and she was...you know. There was a big crowd around them, but nobody was paying a bit of attention to them."

- It was a case of love at first sight for first baseman Norm Zauchin of the Birmingham Barons. In a 1950 game Zauchin chased after a foul pop and fell over the grandstand railing, right into the lap of Janet Mooney. Through the help of an usher, Zauchin found out who the woman was and arranged for dinner at her family's home. A year and a half later the couple married.

More Odds Than Ends

Baseball fans also have been involved in some other bizarre incidents:

- A total of 53 passengers were kicked off a regularly-scheduled America West Airlines flight so the California Angels could return home after their final game of the 1996 season. The club's regular charter plane had mechanical problems, so AWA switched the aircraft.

- It wasn't easy being a Braves fan while the Summer Olympics were staged in Atlanta in 1996. The team was forced to play a 17-game road-trip in 18 days. But one fan, Richey Seaton, the executive director of the Georgia Cotton Commission, knew it was even more difficult on the players. Seaton sent the Braves 50 pairs of underwear and 50 pairs of T-shirts prior to their final series.

- But some other baseball fans have had to go longer without cheering for the home team. In 1994 the Seattle Mariners played 20 road games in 21 days while repairs were made to the Kingdome roof; in 1992 the Houston Astros played 26 road games in 28 days while the Astrodome played host to the Republican national convention; in 1991 the Montreal Expos played 19 road games in 21 days while repairs were made in Olympic Stadium; in 1929 the Boston Braves played 28 straight games on the road; and in 1899 the Cleveland Spiders played 50 straight road games in 52 days.

- Pittsburgh Pirates fans were credited with making a crucial umpiring decision in the second game of the 1909 World Series. Pittsburgh's Dots Miller hit a drive into the right field corner. The ball bounded into the bleachers on one hop. At that time if a ball bounced into the bleachers in fair territory, it was a home run; if it entered the stands in foul territory, it was a double. Said umpire Billy Evans, "I went out to the bleachers to find out if it had (landed in fair territory). I asked the fans, as a group, where the ball landed. One of them proudly held up a ball and answered: 'It landed right here, Mister, and I'm the lad who caught it.'" The lad was sitting in foul territory so the play was ruled a double.

• Home plate was stolen from the Visalia Oaks' Recreation Park in 1996 and held hostage by a disgruntled fan. A woman called the local newspaper and said that the plate was being held until the Oaks snapped their six-game losing streak in the Class A California League. The Oaks went on the road and won, so the same fan called again to say that the plate could be found near the newspaper's building. In the meantime, lacking confidence in its ability to win, the club bought a new home plate. The recovered one was raffled off for charity.

• Ray Collins, a Navy electronics technician stationed in San Diego, was listening to a Padres-Astros game on a headset radio while he mowed his lawn. He was so engrossed in the game that he failed to see his house was on fire. By the time neighbors saw the smoke, the $95,000 home was engulfed in flames.

• Owners of baseball teams open their ball parks so fans can watch their clubs play. But in 1899, Julius Fleischmann was such a fan and so rich, he had a team simply for his own personal enjoyment. The Cincinnati businessman owned a summer home in the Catskills Mountains and spent thousands of dollars to erect what was reportedly the "best base ball field in the country." His Mountain Athletic Base Ball Club was well paid, stayed in a mountain resort and had dressing rooms which featured plunge and shower baths and the first locker room attendant. Fleischmann, who also played a little himself, called on his players to perform on weekends.

• Robert Hunt probably wished he hadn't been first in line to buy tickets for the 1964 World Series in St. Louis. His boss saw Hunt's photograph in the local paper and fired Hunt for skipping work. A bill collector who had been searching for Hunt also saw the photo and caught him. In addition, Hunt was wanted for nonsupport of his family. He was arrested.

• Stanley Tyrkus of Shelby Township, Mich., had his picture taken with Lou Gehrig in front of the visitor's dugout at Detroit's Tiger Stadium at the age of 12. In 1996, 61 years later, Tyrkus had his picture taken with Cal Ripken at Tiger Stadium after Ripken broke Gehrig's record for consecutive games played.

• At Montreal's Jarry Park in 1970, a pair of fans wanted to bring their pet duck to a game. The club had a policy prohibiting dogs and cats, but there wasn't any ban on ducks. So, the fans were asked to buy an extra ticket. When the duck began quacking, fans throughout the stadium started quacking back. After six games, the fans and the duck disappeared.

• Kitty Burke hit a pitch from Daffy Dean in 1935 to become the only woman to bat in a Major League game. However, her at bat doesn't show up in the records book because she wasn't under contract with the hometown Cincinnati Reds. Because of a huge crowd, overflow fans were seated in foul territory along both foul lines. Kitty was only about 10 feet from home plate and began razzing the visiting Cardinals. She shouted at Joe Medwick, "You can't hit a lick. You couldn't even hit the ball with an ironing board." Medwick shot back, "You couldn't hit if you were swinging an elephant." In the bottom of the inning, Kitty beckoned the Reds' Babe Herman. "Hey, Babe, lend me your bat." Kitty, wearing a dress and high heels, walked to the plate and hollered to Dean, "Hey, you hick. Throw me a pitch." The umpire shouted for Dean to play ball, so he lobbed a pitch to the plate. Kitty tapped the ball back to Dean, who tagged her out.

• Joseph Benavides, a 10-year-old from Harlingen, Tex., beat out 50,000 other children in a national essay contest on "Why I Love Baseball," sponsored by Major League Baseball. By winning, Benavides got to attend a 1995 World Series game in Cleveland, his first big-league game. Included in his essay: "There are times when you strike an out, get tagged while running to the base, or maybe even fall. These are things that keep you from going to the next base."

• In 1977, Alan Hartwick, a TV cameraman from Grand Rapids, Mich., wrote to every Major League team — except for the Chicago Cubs — to announce he was becoming the first free-agent fan. He wrote, "I have been a Chicago Cubs fan for 20 years. Whether the score has been Pittsburgh 22, Chicago 0, or Pittsburgh 22, Chicago 1, I have stuck with the Cubs to the

Courtesy of the Baltimore Orioles

Stanley Tyrkus was lucky enough to have his picture taken with Cal Ripken (above) after Ripken broke Lou Gehrig's record.

end. But I don't have a contract with the Cubs' organization. All the Cubs have given me over the years have been a couple of season schedules and games postponed because of darkness. At this moment, I am a fan without a team. I will sign a contract with the ball club that makes the best offer for my services." Hartwick got calls from 10 teams. He accepted the offer from the New Orleans Pelicans, even though it came from a minor league team. The Pelicans flew Hartwick and his wife to New Orleans to throw out the first ball on Opening Day.

• Michael Volpe, a 44-year-old business management consultant from Falls Church, Va., spent 36 years as a San Francisco Giants fan. But in December, 1996, Volpe boxed up his Giants memorabilia and sent it all to the Giants, along with a letter that read, "I am divorcing you and your team from my baseball life. Since California is a community property state, I have decided to part with many of the items acquired during my long-term relationship with the Giants." He then whipped off a letter to the other 27 teams declaring himself a free agent. Since then, Volpe has been contacted by 20 clubs. He pitched to New York Mets manager Bobby Valentine; went on a private tour of Philadelphia's Veterans Stadium, then had dinner with Phillies manager Terry Francona, general manager Lee Thomas and several players; got an offer to appear on a trading card; got to stay at a resort hotel in Miami for three days while he met with Marlins' G.M. Dave Dombroski; was offered a chance to throw out the first pitch at a game in Yankee Stadium; and got a letter from acting commissioner Bud Selig.

• Fittingly, Rick Monday will be remembered long after the names of the fans who made headlines on Apr. 25, 1976. The Chicago Cub was on his way out to center field for the fourth inning in Dodger Stadium. "I saw the creeps run on the field from somewhere down the left field line," Monday recalled. "One of them had something rolled up in his arm. It was a flag. They unfurled it on the grass, like a picnic blanket. One of the idiots took a shiny can out of his pocket. I thought he was dousing it with a flammable liquid, which was the case. The other person whipped out a book of matches. The wind blew the first match out." Monday raced to the scene, snatched the flag and ran away. "The guy threw the can of lighter fluid at me. It missed. I took the flag into foul territory. Doug Rau, a left-handed pitcher with the Dodgers, came out of the dugout and I gave the flag to him." The Dodgers' scoreboard flashed, "Rick Monday...You made a great play." The crowd began singing "God Bless America." The fans — William Thomas of Eldon, Mo., and his 11-year-old son — were protesting the treatment of American Indians during the Bicentennial year. Each was fined $800 and put on probation for two years.

Chapter 3

Basketball

Shortly after basketball was invented in 1891, the court was enclosed by a wire cage, protecting the fans from the players and vice versa. But a wire or rope netting did little to keep fans from jabbing hat pins and lighted cigarettes through the cages at the players' legs. In some cities, fans heated nails and threw them at the referees or opposing players. Most people will say that the game's fans have matured, but after reading these stories...

The Ficker Rule

One fan who National Basketball Association players and coaches wish was behind a cage is Maryland attorney Robin Ficker. The Washington Bullets' season ticket holder might actually be the only fan in professional sports history to have a league enact a rule to control his behavior. Commonly referred to as the "Ficker Rule," the NBA limits the distractions a heckler can create. ("Any spectator who verbally abuses players and/or coaches in a manner which, in the opinion of the game officials, interferes with the ability of a coach to communicate with his players during the game and/or huddles, will, at the direction of the crew chief, be given one warning by a building security officer. If the same spectator continues to behave in a like manner, the crew chief shall direct a building security officer to eject the spectator from the arena.") But Ficker is no ordinary heckler. He's mentioned in the autobiographies of Larry Bird and Charles Barkley. *The Sporting News* once called him, "The most obnoxious, most embarrassing fan in America."

Ficker got tossed out of West Point for "being argumentative about being argumentative." In 1982 he opened a law practice specializing in drunken driving and divorce cases. He served a term in the Maryland House of Delegates.

Since 1985, The Heckler has been sitting in the first row behind the visiting team's bench in Landover, Md., armed with a booming voice. His goal is simple: break a visiting team's concentration. Former Utah Jazz coach Frank Layden tried to attack him; the Golden State Warriors' bench dumped Gatorade on him; and Charles Barkley once grabbed Ficker's poster-board and printed on it, "My name is Robin. I'm retarded."

Ficker has been hired to take his show on the road to opposing arenas. One rule Ficker lives by, though, is not to be rude or vulgar. On a typical night, he might read aloud from a book or newspaper article. (He continues to read passages from the book, *The Jordan Rules*, whenever the Bulls are in town.) He might just yell a player's name. ("The best way to distract players is to keep repeating their names with little variations," he said. "Hare Jordan, Airball Jordan, Airhead Jordan.") He might use props, like a rubber chicken or signs. (After Charles Barkley fouled out of a game, Ficker handed him a T-shirt that read, "I'm having a Maalox moment.") Or he might just be a pest. ("Sit down. Sit down, now! If you don't sit down, I will sit you down!") Through it all, Ficker tries to maintain a sense of humor and hopes the neighboring fans and visiting teams do the same.

 Hecklers don't limit themselves to the players, though. The refs also get a hearty helping of their ire.

- One heckler in Boston couldn't contain himself from going onto the court. An attorney with courtside seats put his red face to within inches of a referee. "As God is my witness, Jess Kersey, you'll roast in hell for that call," he screamed.
- Sid Borgia, a referee in the early days of the NBA, recalls a similar incident. He was officiating a game in Syracuse when

a fan challenged him to call a foul against the Boston Celtics. Borgia's reply brought the fan out of his seat and onto the floor, where they exchanged blows. The fan left without several of his teeth, and Borgia found himself with a $35,000 lawsuit.

- One of the greatest games in NBA history was the triple-overtime fifth game of the 1976 Finals between Boston and Phoenix. At one point, the crowd stormed the floor of Boston Garden, thinking the game had ended. In the confusion, a fan attacked referee Richie Powers. Rather than backing down, Powers fought back. "I think what disturbed Richie the most was that he punched the guy and didn't hurt him," chided Sid Borgia.

- College basketball fans sometimes also get unruly following questionable calls by the officials. In a 1989 game at Oklahoma, fans began throwing objects onto the floor. Sooners coach Billy Tubbs went to the public address announcer's microphone and pleaded with the fans to stop hurling the debris, "regardless of how bad the officiating is." Tubbs was assessed a technical foul.

Nice Guys

While the Utah Jazz' Karl "The Mailman" Malone looks downright mean on a basketball court, off it he is as gentle and caring as he can be. During the 1996 NBA playoffs, he befriended Danny Ewing, a 13-year-old boy with leukemia. Malone met Ewing during a hospital visit and invited the youngster to a game. Malone gave Ewing his jersey, then said after the game: "It's sort of a bittersweet win, because you have people who touch your life throughout this. All

Karl Malone: big guy, big heart.

35

of a sudden you find out certain things, and I have a friend who's not doing too well right now, so this win is for him. He's been my inspiration all year." Said Ewing: "He's a lot better role model than most famous people. He's been a good friend. He's helped brighten my life." Two-and-a-half weeks later, Ewing died. He was buried in his Malone jersey. Malone served as a pallbearer.

Then during a preseason game at Ogden, Utah, Malone observed a woman crying in the front row of the stands. Colleen Grimshaw, a Weber State University police dispatcher, was grieving the death of her daughter's best friend who was killed in an automobile accident. Malone did what he could to cheer her up. He gave her an autographed pair of his size 16 sneakers, along with his wristbands. "It was a sweet gesture," Grimshaw said. "And the shoes did cheer me up, and my daughter as well. I've always been a big fan of Malone's so it's nice to learn that he's really a caring person."

 Malone hasn't cornered the market on helping fans. Many players do what they can to aid fans in need or show appreciation for fan support.

- Karen and Mickey Middleton and their 11 children spent Thanksgiving weekend, 1996, at Walt Disney World in Orlando, complements of the Dallas Mavericks' Jim Jackson. Jackson hooked up with local corporations to fly the entire family to Orlando. He also arranged for hotel accommodations, weekend visits to the theme parks and tickets to the Mavericks' game vs. the Orlando Magic. The Middletons came to Jackson's attention when the family of five adopted eight brothers and sisters who were in need of foster care. "When I first heard about the Middletons, I was stunned at their unselfishness," Jackson said. "Nowadays it's rare when people give of themselves as willingly as Karen and Mickey did. I am totally in awe of their extraordinary example."
- Shaquille O'Neal has helped out three fans by giving them his shoes. No, not to sit on a shelf, but to wear. Shaq had Reebok send a pair of his size 22 sneakers to Allen Joseph, a 6-foot-8 15-year-old in Brampton, Ontario, and size 23 shoes to Josh

Halexa, a 15-year-old in Tacoma, Wash., and Joshua Moore, a 7-foot high school sophomore in Jersey City, N.J.

• Craig Fryar, a 13-year-old Philadelphia 76ers fan, wrote to the team's owner, Pat Croce. He said his Jerry Stackhouse jersey was lost when his family's home burned Feb. 29, 1996. Fryar said he couldn't afford a new Stackhouse jersey when he and his father won tickets and went to the 76ers' opening night game. Croce passed on the letter to Stackhouse, who gave the family free tickets to a game, along with an autographed jersey. Said Stackhouse, "I heard the family had suffered a loss, and I hope this will make Craig's holiday season a little better."

• When Don Nelson was coaching the Golden State Warriors, he came to the rescue of one of the club's biggest fans. Scott Brammeier, then 23 years old, has cerebral palsy and is confined to a wheelchair. He was attending a Warriors' practice and was introduced to David Robinson of the San Antonio

Photos courtesy of the Orlando Magic

Larne Murdoch Photo. Courtesy of the Dallas Mavericks

Shaquille O'Neal and Jim Jackson have both helped special fans.

Spurs, whom Golden State was playing that night. Robinson signed a poster for Brammeier. The young man put the poster in his backpack, but noticed it missing about 15 minutes later. Nelson realized Brammeier was upset, so he investigated the heist. Nelson ran outside the Oakland Coliseum and got on his motorcycle. Security guards pointed him in the direction of two teenagers who were leaving the parking lot. Nelson rode after them and confiscated the poster they had taken. "You don't want to know what I said to them," Nelson said. "I treated them like two of my rookies." Said Brammeier, "He's my friend. If I have problems, Don helps me out."

- Dawn Staley, a national women's basketball player of the year, recorded the biggest assist of her career in 1991. The University of Virginia guard talked a 16-year-old girl from Charlottesville, Va., out of committing suicide. Police, who did not release the girl's name, said she was threatening to jump off a mall's parking garage. When the girl admitted she was a big fan of basketball and Staley, police asked the all-America guard and her coach, Debbie Ryan, to talk to the youth. Staley declined to discuss the incident, but witnesses said she spoke with the girl for several minutes. The girl came down, then talked with Staley and Ryan for two hours more and afterwards, attended some of the team's practices.

Those big players have big hearts, but not everybody is so nice:

- When former Indiana Pacer Malik Sealy was awakened with an early telephone call Apr. 30, 1993, he had no idea what was in store for him. Sealy and the Pacers had arrived in New York the day before, awaiting the start of their first-round NBA playoff series against the Knicks. The team had chartered into Kennedy Airport. When it arrived, Sealy, a native New Yorker, stopped at a pay phone to let relatives know that he was in town. Afterwards, he didn't realize he left a copy of the team's playbook in the phone booth. A short time later, Michael Morrissey, a Bronx fireman, came across the material. A friend persuaded him to give it to WFAN radio shock-jock Don Imus.

To obtain the book, Imus gave Morrissey two tickets to that night's game, along with a $1,000 donation to the Tomorrow's Children's Fund. Imus added his own humorous twists to the scouting report on the Knicks. Said Sealy, "I didn't realize it would wind up in the hands of such tasteless gentlemen."

Fan-atical

One fan who just can't get enough of NBA games visited every arena in the league — twice. John Nordahl, a 26-year-old tour guide at Universal Studios in Orlando, Fla., drove 12,722 miles while spending around $3,400 for lodging and gas during the 1992-93 season. Then he drove 12,367 miles and spent more than $5,400 during the 1994-95 season. The result? An

John Nordahl has visited every NBA arena — twice.

entertaining book, *Traveling, Three Months on the NBA Road* (Macmillan). Among his observations: The best dance team is the Laker Girls; the best mascot is Denver's Rocky; a total of 26 arenas serve Coke, 3 serve Pepsi; and the four best arenas are in New York, Orlando, Phoenix and Utah.

 That's fanatical, but he's not alone. Many fans are over-zealous in their love of basketball.

- Phoenix Suns fans take their basketball seriously. Just ask Tom O'Neill, manager of the HiLiter Showcase, a topless bar. "We have to put the Suns' playoff games on TV, or we lose most of our customers at tip-off," he said. "As it is, we still lose a bunch. I guess during the game, they don't want any distractions."
- Takashi and Rika Kuroda, of Nara, Japan, are big Chicago Bulls fans. How big? They flew 6,200 miles from Japan to Chi-

cago just to have their wedding reception at a Bulls game.

- But Chicago sports fans can get out of hand. Following the Bulls' 1993 NBA championship, two people were killed and nearly 700 arrested during the night-long celebrations. Julio Castillo, an 18-year-old passenger in a car, was pulled out of the vehicle, shot and killed. Rosalind Slaughter, 26, died when she was hit by a stray bullet while standing on a porch outside her home. Following the club's 1992 title, more than 1,000 people were arrested, 107 police officers were injured and damage to property exceeded $10 million. In 1996, city officials considered it calm when "only" 650 people were arrested and 38 stores were looted or broken into.

- Georgetown's Allen Iverson was the No. 1 pick in the 1996 NBA draft. But the 6-foot guard's checkered past caused Hampton, Va., Mayor James L. Eason to receive criticism for staging a parade to honor the hometown player. Thousands of fans took part in the festivities, including one lone protester, Sandra Radford. She held a sign, "Millions don't make a hero, morals do." Iverson was convicted in 1993 on mob violence charges for his role in a bowling alley fracas, but the conviction later was overturned.

- Kansas State University students got in line for the school's season tickets on Oct. 8, 1987, even though it hadn't been announced when tickets would go on sale. Soon there were 50 tents of various shapes and colors. Each was manned 24-hours-a-day by teams of six students. A week later, officials announced that tickets would go on sale Oct. 26, but when the temperature dropped into the 20's, administrators feared for the students' health. The date was moved up to Oct. 23. During the final night, KSU coach Lon Kruger and his players served 300 bowls of chili to the students in line.

- Fans at Central Michigan University have a tradition. When the Chippewas score their first home basket each season, nearly every fan in attendance hurls a roll of toilet paper onto the court. Mid-American Conference officials, naturally, weren't too thrilled with the delays, but the fans vowed to continue the tradition. "The place goes crazy," said one student. "This is what college basketball is supposed to be!"

The first home point of the season at Central Michigan University.

Mob Rule

Southern Utah University fans learned a tough lesson about decorum in a 1996 game vs. Weber State. SUU was trailing by two points when it fouled Weber's Bryan Emery with four seconds left. Emery missed the first free throw. Before he could attempt his second toss, a fan threw a quarter-sized, plastic object at Emery. The referees had issued the fans a warning earlier in the game, so they called a technical foul on the SUU supporters. Emery made his free throw, then Jimmy DeGraffenreid made both technical shots to seal the victory. Upset fans pelted the officials and players with ice and garbage as they left the court.

 That's not the only time the crowd has influenced the outcome of a game. Get a load of these fans:

• In a 1980 game at the University of New Mexico, the Lobos lost because of their rowdy fans. New Mexico had a 70-69 lead over the University of Texas-El Paso with two seconds remaining in the game. UTEP's Wayne Campbell was at the free throw line to shoot a one-and-one. Just as he shot his first free throw, a paper cup flew past his line of sight. The shot was no good and Campbell should have lost his opportunity for a second shot, likely giving New Mexico a victory. But the referee ruled the free throw didn't count, because of the paper cup. Campbell got to repeat his first toss and made the shot. Now entitled to the second free throw, he made that, too, to give UTEP a 71-70 victory.

• At Wichita State University in 1952, rowdy fans prevented the Shockers from a possible overtime in a game against Drake. WSU's old arena, The Forum, had a balcony that practically hung out over the court. With the score tied at 63, Drake was working for a last-second shot. Just before the buzzer sounded, Drake threw up a shot, but a fan in the balcony tossed his coat over the basket, preventing the ball from going in. Recalled referee Alex George, "The Drake coach was screaming that the shot had to count, and the Wichita coach was yelling that it shouldn't count because the ball wouldn't have gone in the basket anyway. I didn't do anything at first, because all those fans were right on top of us and about to tear the building down. Cliff Ogden (the other official) ran over to me and asked, 'Well, Alex, what are you going to call it?' I said, 'How far are we away from our dressing room door?' He said, 'About 100 feet.' 'The basket has to count, but if I tell them now, we'll never make it out of here with our skins.' We ran to the dressing room door, and I turned around and yelled, 'Good!' Then we locked ourselves inside while objects of every kind came flying out from the balcony and a screaming mob covered the court."

• Rutgers University students have a tradition of using college basketball games to stage protests. In 1973 and 1980 against Pittsburgh, protesting minority students disrupted play and forced the suspension of the games. Then on Feb. 7, 1995, at halftime of the Rutgers-Massachusetts game, student protesters struck again. First one female student walked out of the stands to center court and sat down. With both teams on their benches, ready to begin the second half, she was joined by more than 100 other students. The protesters joined hands, unfurled banners and, as the crowd booed, directed chants at Dr. Francis

L. Lawrence, Rutgers' president. The protest was in response to remarks about minority students made by Lawrence. Linda Bruno, the commissioner of the Atlantic 10 Conference, was in attendance, and after conferring with the coaches and school officials, postponed the game.

- Fans at Texas Tech took out their frustration over a 1994 loss on the opposing coach, Tony Barone, Jr., of Texas A&M. Seconds after A&M's 89-88 victory, fans blocked the ramp to A&M's dressing room. Four fans charged Barone. One yelled obscenities, then tried to hit the coach, but was knocked unconscious by a punch from A&M player Joe Wilbert. Other fans joined in the melee, knocking down A&M player David Edwards, before order was restored.

 Fans aren't the only ones prone to violence. Sometimes the athletes get into the act, too:

- Trail Blazers fan Steve George was punched in the jaw by the Houston Rockets' Vernon Maxwell in a 1995 game at Portland. Maxwell ran 12 rows into the stands to get at George. George and his brother, Nick, said they were shouting, "Five points and four fouls — nice game." Maxwell claims he was reacting to racial slurs, profanities and remarks about his daughter, who died at birth. Maxwell was fined $20,000 and suspended for 10 games by the NBA. George filed a $4.5 million lawsuit, but later agreed to an out-of-court settlement.
- Dennis Rodman got into a scuffle with an autograph-seeking fan following a 1995 playoff game in Los Angeles. Steve Coakley, a 24-year-old Long Beach waiter, said, "I was just trying to get an autograph, and I had a pen in one hand and (the game program) in the other." Witnesses said Rodman, who accused Coakley of taunting him, got Coakley in a headlock before a teammate intervened.
- Charles Barkley has had his share of skirmishes with fans. A recent one was in Cleveland during the summer of 1996. Barkley was in town with his Dream Team III Olympic teammates, preparing for an exhibition game against Brazil. Barkley

was accused of punching Jeb Tyler in the nose at The Basement, a Cleveland bar. Tyler, 23, of Spencerport, N.Y., filed a complaint accusing Barkley of assault, then later filed a $50,000 lawsuit. Barkley said Tyler made a lewd comment to a woman who was with him, and Tyler attacked him. Barkley filed a report accusing Tyler of using bodily force against him.

Barkley was acquitted of charges he hit a fan in the face during a game at New Jersey in 1992. New York fireman Dennis McKeever alleged Barkley punched and knocked him out as he reached toward Barkley to congratulate him on a good game. Barkley's attorney argued the all-star forward was deflecting what he believed was an oncoming blow from an irate sports fan.

Charges were dropped against Barkley and teammate Jayson Williams after they were accused of being in a bar fight in Chicago in 1992. Earlier that year, Barkley was acquitted of misdemeanor battery and disorderly conduct charges for punching a man who had taunted him and a friend outside a Milwaukee bar. The jury accepted Barkley's argument that he acted in self-defense when he broke the Milwaukee man's nose.

 In a side note, Barkley's past didn't prevent Duncan Shirley from coveting the all-star's shoes. During an interview on NBC during the 1996 Olympics, Shirley recalled the sneaker the Dream Teamer threw into the stands, caught by his son: "Overwhelming excitement. Adrenaline. Just pure excitement. It's just a father's dream for a child."

• And finally, one of the most volatile basketball coaches is Indiana University's Bob Knight. On March 28, 1981, during the NCAA Final Four weekend at Philadelphia, Knight had a verbal and physical exchange with LSU fan Louis Bonnecaze, Jr. The incident occurred at the Cherry Hill (N.J.) Inn, just hours after Indiana had beaten LSU in the semifinals. A newspaper report said Bonnecaze called Knight "a jack--- and Knight physically picked him up and threw him back, and (Bonnecaze) fell into a garbage can." Responded Knight, "The headline reads,

'Knight trades shoves, insults with LSU fan.' We didn't trade shoves, because I did all the shoving, and we didn't trade insults, because he did all the insulting. What happened was this. With four or five other people, I was walking through a lounge adjacent to the dining room when this person walked by me and said, 'Congratulations.' I saw he was dressed in purple and gold, and I took him for an LSU fan. All morning Saturday, their fans kept chanting, 'Tiger bait, Tiger bait, there goes our Tiger bait,' when our players walked from meeting rooms to the breakfast room and back. Well, the Tigers got ahold of us, but they couldn't swallow the bait. As I walked past, I turned to him and said over my shoulder, 'We weren't really Tiger bait after all, were we?' and I kept on walking. The guy went toward the door, turned to me and shouted, 'A--hole, Knight's an a--hole.' I walked over — I did a little more than walk over, I walked swiftly over — and said, 'Would you like to say again what you just said?' He said, 'I gave you a compliment and you were very rude and sarcastic to me. You're still an a--hole.' With the next word he was saying, he was sitting on his a--. I grabbed him, shoved him against the wall, turned and walked away. Now, if a guy calls me an a--hole three or four times in front of 100 people, and the guy is a total stranger to me, and if I walk over to him and shove him against the wall, if what I did was wrong, then so be it. If it happens again tomorrow, then I'll be wrong again tomorrow." Later Knight said, "In most situations I act very disciplined, but in that incident I failed in reaching the ultimate discipline. Society is so tolerant to so many things these days that it is not a particularly good omen for the direction this country is going. The license fans believe they have to utter obscenities to players, coaches and officials is a real cancer to athletics."

Football

Dawgs Without A Home

Perhaps the best known football fans don't have anyone to cheer for right now. They're the Cleveland Dawg Pound who watched in dismay in the spring of 1996 as the Cleveland Browns moved to Baltimore. The Dawg Pound was located in the end zone seats at Municipal Stadium and was known for its antics that included dressing up like dogs, barking like dogs and chewing on bones like dogs. In a 1978 game against Houston, the then unorganized group forced the officials to move the ball to the opposite end of the stadium when players were pelted with snowballs and trash. In a 1989 game vs. Denver, the Dawgs threw so many batteries, dog biscuits and eggs onto the turf that the officials again moved the two teams to the other end of the field. Because of that move, the Browns' Matt Bahr booted a 48-yard game-winning field goal with the wind at his back that, according to Bahr, "cleared the crossbar by one or two coats of paint." Following that game, stadium officials attempted to crack down on the Pound and issued a 10-point program to reduce rowdiness. It included video surveillance of the crowd, restrictions on beer sales and a ban on eggs, rocks, dog biscuits and any other items that could be thrown onto the field. Bones — foam or real — also were barred. Despite those measures, the Dawgs still managed to create havoc.

The group got its name — and identity — in 1984 when Browns cornerback Hanford Dixon labeled his defensive unit "The Dawg

Cleveland Stadium used to be home to the Dawg Pound, which filled the end zone.

Defense." He began barking at opponents and urged the rowdy end zone fans to do likewise.

When the city of Cleveland staged a national campaign to keep their Browns, one of the Pound's own was in the center spotlight. John "Big Dawg" Thompson — wearing a Browns jersey, orange shoes and a dog collar — testified at a hearing in front of the U.S. House of Representative's Judiciary Committee. "I'm just one fan," Thompson said. "There are hundreds of thousands of NFL fans across the country that have the same investments that I do and also the same feelings."

Not wanting to get out of practice waiting for the NFL to move a team to Cleveland, the Dawg pound "rented" itself to the Buffalo Bills for a game against the hated Cincinnati Bengals in 1996. More than 2,000 fans, led by "Big Dawg" Thompson, journeyed to Buffalo from Cleveland.

> *Browns fans aren't the only ones without a team. Fans at the California Institute of Technology have remained rabid despite the school giving up football in 1977. Caltech compiled a record of 107-322 through the years, but that didn't stop the students from wishing their intelligent comrades well. One cheer was: Secant, cosine, tangent, sine Logarithm, logarithm, Hyperbolic sine 3 point 1 4 1 5 1 9 Slipstick, slide rule TECH, TECH, TECH!*

• But even with a poor performance by the team on the field, the students still had an impact on the game. You see, Caltech students are known for staging elaborate pranks, and one of their targets was the annual Rose Bowl game played across town. At the 1961 Rose Bowl between Minnesota and Washington, a group of 14 Caltech students sabotaged Washington's famed student card section. The card flashers created colorful, animated signs during halftime of Husky games. The Caltech students stole an instruction sheet for one of the stunts, reprogrammed it, made 2,232 duplicate copies and then watched as stunts 10, 11, and 12 were performed. Instead of "Washington," stunt 10 became "Caltech." Instead of "Huskies," stunt 11 became "seiksuh." And instead of a drawing of a Husky, stunt 12 became a drawing of the Caltech mascot, a beaver.

- The Caltech students stayed away from the Rose Bowl until 1984 when they were able to take control of the stadium's electronic scoreboard via a remote control in a van nearly a mile away. After a couple of minor adjustments to test the system, the Techies finally changed the board to read: Caltech 38, MIT 9. The Rose Bowl officials, sensing the worst, completely turned off the scoreboard.

Watch Those Snowballs

The "Dawg Pound" may have started with a snowball fight, but they haven't been the only group of fans to engage in snowy battles. Anyone can have a little fun with his friends. But don't ever get into a snowball fight at a football game in Giants Stadium at East Rutherford, N.J. That's what Jeffrey Lange did at a 1995 Giants game, and his photograph appeared in nearly every newspaper in the nation with the headline: "Wanted!" Lange, 26, of Bridgewater, N.J., became the poster child of hundreds of fans who threw snowballs that day when he was

This photo of Jeffrey Lange appeared in papers across the country.

captured on film by an Associated Press photographer. Lange was identified by about 20 callers seeking a $1,000 reward. Nearly 200 people were ejected from the stadium, and 15 fans were arrested when the snowball fight got out of hand. San Diego Chargers equipment manager Sid Brooks was knocked unconscious from a blow. The Giants purchased a full-page newspaper ad in the San Diego *Union-Tribune*, apologizing to Chargers officials and fans. Among those arrested was a teacher, who attended the game with his wife and two daughters, and a retired police chief. The Giants revoked the season tickets of fans who were ejected. "I feel like I'm being tossed out there like a piece of meat to the lions," said Lange. "Honestly, I can't believe I've been singled out." Lange eventually was convicted of improper behavior, fined $500 and forced to pay $150 more in court fees and other costs.

Another snowball actually affected the outcome of an NFL game, but the thrower got away...

- It was thrown Nov. 11, 1985, in Denver's Mile High Stadium. As the San Francisco 49ers were attempting a 19-yard field goal at the end of the first half, a snowball hit the turf in front of holder Matt Cavanaugh just as he was receiving the snap. He dropped the ball and was forced to scramble, throwing an incomplete pass. Denver eventually won the Monday night game, 17-16, but not before more than 50 fans had been ejected for throwing snowballs. The *San Francisco Examiner* offered a $500 reward for the snowball thrower to come forward and tell his story. He contacted the newspaper, but did not reveal his name or accept the money. He did offer this insight: "It just happened on the spur of the moment. Me and my buddy both threw snowballs at the same time. His hit the left upright and mine bounced in front of Cavanaugh. Everybody around us started calling us jerks. That's when I realized it was stupid. I'm really sorry about what I did, and I want to apologize to the 49ers and the 49er fans. I don't want the money. I feel bad enough already. Everybody thinks I'm a jerk."

Disgruntled Fans

In 1948 at Baltimore Stadium, the Colts were playing the Buffalo Bills in the All-American Football Conference playoffs. The Bills scored the game-winning touchdown late in the game after a controversial call by head linesman Tommy Whelan. Following the game, about 1,000 fans swarmed the field and attacked Whelan, giving him a swollen eye, a ripped shirt and a torn cap before players from both teams rescued him. The fans refused to leave the stadium and threw bottles and garbage on the field. Meanwhile, Whelan escaped by hiding on the Bills' team bus. Fans became so outraged that they set fire to the west side of the stadium. The blaze was extinguished and the stadium finally evacuated.

 Fortunately, most unhappy fans vent their frustrations in less violent ways...

- An unhappy fan in St. Louis in the 1970s bought an ad in the local newspaper offering "a playbook illustrating all FIVE of the Cardinals offensive plays, including the squib punt."
- In 1978, New York Giants fan Ron Freiman of Livingston, N.J., took out an ad urging season ticket holders to cut up their tickets and send them to him to fuel a bonfire outside the stadium at the next home game. A group of fans ran its own ad, calling for a mass protest rally to show management they were "mad as hell and not going to take it anymore." A plane pulled a banner over the stadium that read, "15 yrs. of lousy football. We've had enough." That prompted the fans in the stands to chant: "We've had enough! We've had enough!"
- Meanwhile, a disgruntled fan in Atlanta in 1979 tried to give away a pair of tickets to strangers in a shopping mall. When no one would take them, he put them under the windshield wiper of his car, hoping someone would take them while he shopped. When he returned to his vehicle, he found the two tickets still there — along with four more.

When Fans And Players Collide

Fans who venture near the field of play do so at their own risk. In December, 1971, Donald Ellis, 30, of Rochester, N.Y., was watching the host Baltimore Colts play the Miami Dolphins. In the second half Ellis jumped over the stadium's guard rail, ran onto the field, grabbed the football while the two teams were huddled between plays, and then ran for the opposite sideline. "My friends didn't think I would do it," said Ellis. "I didn't know I would do it either, but suddenly I was out there." Colts linebacker Mike Curtis wasn't humored. He raced after Ellis and leveled him with a fore-arm to the back of the neck. Said Curtis, "I believe in law and order. That fellow had no right on the field. I felt it was in line to make him aware of his wrongdoing. I couldn't take the idea of people getting in my way when I was doing my job." Ellis was taken to a hospital, then to the Baltimore Municipal Court Build-ing where he was charged with disorderly conduct. Later Ellis sued Curtis and the Colts for $250,000, claiming he was attacked "without provocation."

 Most fan-sports celebrity meetings are positive experiences, but when emotions are high, things can get out of control. Take at look at these examples...

• Chicago Bears coach Mike Ditka had his share of run-ins with fans, too. In 1987 at San Francisco, Ditka was running off the field at halftime and wasn't pleased with the way 49ers fans treated the Bears. A police report described Ditka's reaction: "As I was escorting Coach Ditka from the playing field, he stopped and looked at the people sitting in the pullout seats. He then took a piece of gum from his mouth and threw it at victim-reportee Terry Ornelas, striking her in the back of the head. Coach Ditka then flipped the bird and exited the field." Ornelas, 38, of Napa, Calif., got the gum stuck in her hair. The wad was displayed at police headquarters two days later. Ditka claimed fans were throwing ice at him and his players. "Any time somebody throws something at me, I'm going to throw something back," he said.

• Buddy Ryan, then the head coach of the Philadelphia Eagles, nearly choked to death on a pork chop in 1988. When the Eagles went to Dallas shortly thereafter, fans — still angry at Ryan for running up the score of a 1987 game — pelted Ryan with pork chops. The local media dubbed the game "The Pork Chop Bowl."

- Following the 49ers-Packers 1997 playoff game in Green Bay, William Scharlas of Waukesha, Wis., claims he was head-butted by 49ers owner Edward DeBartolo, Jr. Scharlas, 30, told the Green Bay *Press-Gazette* that he was standing with about 30 other fans outside the Lambeau Field gate, waiting for the 49ers players to come out to heckle them. "Everybody was yelling '40-whiners' and things like that," he said. "One guy came out, a big guy. They opened the gate for him, and the next thing I knew, he head-butted me." Witnesses told police DeBartolo punched a fan, who fell backward over a garbage can. Another man, later identified as Edward Muransky of Atherton, Calif., allegedly head-butted another fan. DeBartolo and Muransky were charged with battery and fined $500 plus $140 in court costs. Scharlas and Dale Nault were cited for disorderly conduct in the scuffle.

- Place-kicker Greg Davis was a rookie with the Atlanta Falcons when he stopped to sign an autograph for a fan after practice. A few days later, he received a call at home from the same fan who said he was waiting in a telephone booth around the corner to give Davis a birthday present. Davis stopped by and was presented with a trophy and plaque, proclaiming him the NFL's greatest kicker, and a book of poems. He turned over the plaque and saw that it was signed, "Love, Tim." Davis no longer accepts gifts from fans, male or female.

- NFL veteran Ron Wolfley has figured out the difference between fans: "The only thing that separates them is what they throw. On the west coast, they throw food. The farther east you move, the larger and harder the objects become. In Midwest cities like Chicago, it's an AA battery. When you get to Philadelphia, it's a D battery."

Taking A Loss A Little Too Hard

- In Kansas City, 35 fans signed up for Chiefs Grief, a therapy session designed to help people get over the team's Jan. 7, 1996, playoff loss to the Indianapolis Colts.

- In New York, after the Jets got off to a 0-4 start in the 1996 season, the *New York Daily News* conducted a contest. It asked despondent fans to write a letter describing their misery and how it has affected their lives. Eight letter writers were awarded with a group therapy session with Frederick Kass, head of the psychiatric division at New York's Columbia Presbyterian Medical Center.
- Another fan, 30-year-old Tony Morelli, of Wintersville, Ohio, drove his car through a set of gates at Three Rivers Stadium in Pittsburgh in 1987, knocked down several tubs of nacho cheese sauce and drove up the interior stadium ramps before stopping on the third level. He abandoned his car, ran down to the playing field and pretended to kick game-winning field goals until police interrupted him. Said officer Frank Vetere: "He just said he was tired of (Steelers' quarterback) Mark Malone's passing."

Here's proof, though, that football can help the psychologically troubled:

- From the *Chicago Journal*, Nov. 10, 1903: "Enthusiasm aroused at a football game accomplished for an aged woman patient at Dunning what ten years of treatment failed to do. From the time she was entered at the asylum the woman never spoke, refusing to ever answer questions of her attendants. She sat in her chair day after day, with stooped shoulders and bowed head. Her eyes were generally half closed, and she was apparently sleeping her life away. Physicians had given up all hope of breaking her melancholic state.

  "The awakening came two weeks ago at a football game between the St. Vincent college and Oak Park high school teams. Supt. Podstata favors allowing the patients to witness a football game or dance, occasionally, believing such amusement is beneficial to them. Along with scores of crippled men and deaf and dumb women the silent patient's chair was arranged so the occupant could scan the 'gridiron.' The game was a spectacular one, and there was much cheering. Slowly but surely a change came over the melancholy woman. She straightened her shoulders, raised her head, and astonished the crippled woman sitting beside her by saying:

"'What a degree of excitement attends this contest?'

"Since then she has talked almost continually, the dullness in her eyes has vanished, and a tinge of ruddy pink has begun to appear in her sallow cheeks."

• Brent Doyle of Broomfield, Colo., crashed his motorcycle as an 18-year-old in 1988. He suffered head injuries and was in a coma. Doyle was a big Miami Dolphins fan, so friends, along with Denver broadcaster Mike Nolan, arranged for Dan Marino to record a tape of encouragement. Doyle's father, Don, played the tape for his son every day. On it, Marino said, "Come on. You can snap out of it. All of the Dolphins are behind you 100 percent." A month later, Doyle emerged from the coma and returned home.

Young Fans

• Jeffrey Grant is an 8-year-old 49er fan living in Austin, Tex. To celebrate a San Francisco win over the nearby Dallas Cowboys, he and his 5-year-old brother, Alexander, let loose two helium-filled balloons from their home. The balloons carried the message, "Go 49ers — Super Bowl!" and their telephone number. The next night the family got a call from a man who had found one of the balloons in his backyard — in London, Ohio.

• Another youngster, Larry Champagne III of St. Louis, Mo., was named the Most Valuable Player on the 1995-96 All-Madden Team. The annual award, given by FOX analyst John Madden, went to the 10-year-old for saving his fellow classmates on a school bus after the driver suffered a stroke. He saw the driver fall from her seat, made his way to the front of the bus, grabbed the steering wheel and stomped on the break.

• Another 10-year-old, Trey Brandon Davis of Jacksonville, Fla., was selected in a random drawing and got to play a sandlot football game featuring Dan Marino and Jeff Blake. The game was video-taped and highlights were shown during the 1997 Super Bowl telecast.

A Romantic Candlelight Football Game

A football game was responsible for Chuck Barris getting married. A seemingly simple $50 bet on the Oakland Raiders-San Diego Chargers game in 1980 mushroomed into a final-minute come-from-behind plea to the radio and his girlfriend, Red: "I promise on my word of honor, on my mother's life, on the lives of my sister's children, if (Jim) Plunkett completes a touchdown pass...I'll marry you." Plunkett completed the TD pass, and the couple was married. The Raiders got word of the promise and considered Red their good luck charm. The club even invited her to the Super Bowl.

As you may have suspected, football doesn't help a lot of relationships:

- This couple might not make it to the altar: Kansas City Chiefs fan Chris Russert challenged anyone at her engagement party to trade punches with her so she could prove she was tougher than former Houston Oilers assistant coach Buddy Ryan. Lee Walters took the dare and knocked her backward with a punch to the right side of her face. She then punched him in the face and broke his nose. Lee Walters was her fiancé.
- This couple probably didn't watch any more football games together: In 1990, Viola Delores Douglas, an unemployed nurse in Houston, was watching a Disney movie on TV when her fiancé, Eddie Harris, returned to the apartment they shared. He switched the TV to another channel so he could watch the Super Bowl. According to police reports, Douglas was infuriated. She attacked Harris with a knife, but he disarmed her. Douglas left the room, but when she returned, she found that Harris wasn't paying attention to the TV. Douglas attacked Harris again, this time with a barbecue fork. A wound to Harris' neck required several stitches. Douglas was sentenced to 10 months in jail after pleading guilty to misdemeanor assault.
- And this pair may not make it for long: A newlywed couple, dressed as if they came straight from the wedding chapel to Lambeau Field, site of the Green Bay Packers-San Diego Chargers game, held up a sign, "Just married. First fight." The groom was wearing a cheesehead, the bride a Chargers bolt.

Fans Are Good Business

Speaking of cheeseheads, a Packers fan credits the foam head-gear with helping save his life. Frank Emmert, Jr., was wearing his cheesehead when the light plane he was riding in crashed. Now it goes wherever he goes. "I cleaned it up so it's not that bad. I'll even put it in my checklist. 'Cheese — check.'"

• Packers' fans, like all NFL teams, can choose from a wide variety of unique novelty items. But only in Green Bay can fans get a Packer Backer Tractor. Simplicity Manufacturing Inc. of Port Washington, Wis., made fewer than 500 specially painted lawn mowers complete with a face guard on the grille and a uniform number on the body. The green and gold grass cutters retail for $3,000-$3,500.

Photo courtesy of Foamation Inc.

• If "real men don't eat quiche," then a home-furnishings store chain probably would

From Cheese-heads to the Packer Backer Tractor, Green Bay fans support their team.

Photo courtesy of Simplicity Manufacturing, Inc.

have gone broke on Jan. 15, 1995. IKEA offered free quiche to all males who visited its stores the same day as the NFL conference championships, "to give a break to the men who turn off the game and spend their Sundays creating beautiful things."

Fan v. Fan

In 1995, surgeons tried unsuccessfully to reattach a football fan's ear after an Oakland Raiders fan bit it off during a bar room brawl. Michael Burrows, 45, was at Fat Freddie's in San Diego, watching the San Diego Chargers-Philadelphia Eagles game on TV. Carl Anthony Ditmars, 30, an avid Raiders fan, didn't take kindly to Burrows' teasing that the Raiders had lost to Kansas City that day. Police said Ditmars allegedly attacked Burrows, then bit off a 2-inch by 1-inch piece of Burrows' ear in the scuffle. Ditmars was held by other bar patrons until police arrived. He pleaded guilty to a felony battery charge.

- Following a Packers' victory over the Bears, Chicago fans dragged a Green Bay fan out of a bar near the Wisconsin-Illinois border and duct-taped him to a stop sign under a placard that said, "Packers Fan."
- Fans of the Jacksonville Jaguars didn't like the way Woody Paige, a columnist for *The Denver Post*, referred to the team as the "Jagwads." So, following the Jaguars' upset victory over the Broncos in the 1996 playoffs, a Jacksonville TV station scrolled Paige's computer address across the screen. He was bombarded by fans' taunts. "My voicemail is full. My e-mail must have 3,000 messages," Paige said. "I can't even get in, because as soon as I sign on, I get hundreds of instant messages saying, 'Talk to me!'"

The same Jacksonville fans also can show their appreciation. Hundreds of fans have sent thank you cards and letters to Morten Andersen, the Atlanta Falcons' kicker, who missed a last-second 30-yard field goal in the final game of the 1996 season that enabled the Jaguars to qualify for the playoffs. "There were a lot of 'thank you' cards, some really creative letters and a couple of borderline stabs," he said. "I received some cash ($5) and a check from someone wanting my autograph. I guess that was my cut of the playoff money."

Fans And Strategy

The San Francisco 49ers are famous for scripting the first 15-20 offensive plays of every game. Bill Walsh, now an administrative assistant with the club, began the practice in 1979 when he was the head coach. It was Walsh, though, who gave the list of plays for a 1996 Monday night game in Green Bay to a Packers fan. Walsh was signing an autograph for a woman on a napkin the night before the game when he accidentally gave her the papers containing the plays. The woman, who refused to be identified, said she thought about returning the sheets to Walsh when she realized what she had, but was convinced by a friend to take them to the Packers. She said her friend took them to the team's offices Monday morning. Did the Packers use the info? No one knows for sure, but the 49ers did not score in the first quarter and made only two first downs on their first 19 offensive plays, and one of them came on a busted play.

 One fan had the opportunity to fulfill every armchair quarterback's dream...

• The Oakland Raiders took the advice of a season ticket holder in beating the Jacksonville Jaguars in 1996. Roy Nagy, a season ticket holder from Stockton, Calif., sent a letter to owner Al Davis, head coach Mike White and special teams coach Rusty Tillman, suggesting a fake punt he once saw. And the Raiders ran the play. "When he sent it to me, it got the wheels turning," said Tillman. "I called him and said he could take the credit if it worked, and I'd take the heat if it didn't work." The idea of Nagy's play was to make a pass look like a punt. "I saw it run about 15-20 years ago," said Nagy. "I kept thinking to myself, 'Why doesn't somebody use this again?' I'd had the play in my mind for the last year or so. I just knew it would work." The Raiders tried the play from the Jacksonville 38-yard line in the second quarter of the scoreless game. Punter Jeff Gossett took the snap and put both hands on the ball, as if preparing to kick. Then he crouched and lofted a high, long pass down the sideline. Raiders receiver Kenny Shedd battled Jacksonville's Vinnie Clark as the ball fell to the ground. Both players were called for pass interference. The offsetting penalties wiped out the play. "I told Roy it was a hell of an idea," said Tillman. "We did it the way he suggested. It's kind of fun to get letters from fans. I just don't want any hate mail."

 Some fans' strategy is more out of control. The following are examples of how not to support your favorite team...

• A Tennessee fan in 1908 wasn't too pleased his Volunteers were about to be scored on by the Georgia Bulldogs. He walked out of the stands and into the Georgia huddle. He pulled out a .38-caliber revolver and proclaimed, "The first man who crosses that goal line will get a bullet in his carcass." The man was escorted off the field by the authorities. But Georgia fumbled on the next play and lost to Tennessee, 10-0.

• Fans contributed to the cancellation of a 43-year-old tradition, the College All-Star Football Game. It was July 23, 1976, and the all-stars were playing the Pittsburgh Steelers in Chicago's Soldier Field. A lightning storm in the third quarter forced the game to be delayed, but thousands of fans went on the rain-soaked field to slide around in the muck. A gang of fans even tore down the goal posts and pointed them skyward as lightning rods. Fans began playing their own game and refused to leave the field. After 20 minutes, the players retreated to the dressing rooms, and the game was called off. A line of more than 100 policemen finally forced the fans off the field. But the game's organizers had seen enough and canceled the game, forever.

• Brawls in the stands during the fourth quarter marred the 1996 Hawaii-Brigham Young game in Honolulu. One fan was arrested for disorderly conduct and several others were ejected from the stadium. Hawaii quarterback Glenn Freitas raced into the stands to defend his father, who was attacked. In a separate incident, the wife of Hawaii coach Fred vonAppen had her lip cut when she was punched in the mouth while trying to play peacemaker. Redshirt running back Quincy Jacobs also was attacked while he tried to protect Mrs. vonAppen.

• West Virginia fans created a stir in 1996 when they rocked and almost tipped over an ambulance that was carrying an injured Miami player to the hospital. At the same game, Miami assistant coach Randy Shannon was knocked to the ground and bruised when he was struck by a trash can hurled from the stands. Said UWV President David Hardesty, "The vast majority of our students and fans were well behaved. But we obviously have a minority that was intent on behaving in a way that hurt us all. And I'm very disappointed."

Coaches Are Fans, Too

The 1st Poinsettia Bowl had an attendance problem in 1952. NBC Sports was scheduled to televise the game from San Diego's Balboa Stadium. The only problem was a day-long torrential rain forced most fans to stay home. NBC officials didn't want to go on the air with an empty stadium, so they sought the help of the Navy Shore Patrol. The Patrol raided bars, cafes and movie theaters issuing orders for all servicemen to go to the game. The soldiers that could be found huddled into one section for the benefit of televised "crowd" shots. One of those fans was Hayden Fry, now the head football coach at the University of Iowa. "We heard we were there to play the crowd scene," Fry said. "But at the time, none of us knew why we were sitting there in a downpour. The Shore Patrol just picked us up, took us to the stadium, and told us to enjoy the game. Some enjoyment."

• Fry's Iowa fans find their own ways to enjoy the games. Among them is stealing the helmets from visiting quarterbacks. In 1995, thieves got away with opponents' headgear in consecutive weeks, against Indiana and Penn State. According to Penn State QB Doug Ostrosky, "It was on the bench, and I turned around and it was gone. I saw a guy flying up the stairs of the stadium with my helmet." The Indiana QB (who remained anonymous) said his helmet was sitting under the Hoosier bench. "The next thing you know, the quarterback says, 'My helmet is gone,'" said Marty Clark, Indiana's equipment manager. "Same thing. Exact same thing."

• But Fry had other things to complain about. He was disgusted with Iowa fans who threw beer cans, liquor bottles and animal parts on the field during games. "Lock 'em up," Fry said. "It's just ridiculous. The police need to come down on them. Lock their tails up. The more they get away with, the more they're going to do. It's really gotten dangerous. I imagine if I got hit upside the head with a beer can, I'd probably want to go up in the stands and offer the beer right back in their mouth." Police arrested 10 people at one game vs. Penn State and ejected another 41 fans.

• Fry also has complained that football crowds have become too noisy. He's suggested the use of sound meters to determine if the home crowd is disrupting the opponent. In one Iowa game, *Sports Illustrated* took sound readings and determined that the Hawkeye crowd reached 102 decibels, the equivalent of a circular saw.

That's not nearly as bad as the noise in an Iowa-Iowa State game in 1905. Iowa's engineering students rigged a steam engine that emitted a piercing whistle. With cotton in their ears, the engineers blared their whistle every time Iowa State had the ball. None of the Cyclones could hear their quarterback's signals, and Iowa State failed to score the entire game. After the Iowa win, officials confiscated the whistle, and it was never used again.

Dedicated Fans

Chuck Moore was once the only fan who bought a ticket the day of a major college football game. It was Nov. 12, 1955, and Washington State was playing host to San Jose. The weather was unseasonably bad, even for the Northwest. It was five degrees above zero; a bitter wind and snow made visibility zero. A total of 400 people braved the cold weather, but the other 399 were season ticket holders or members of the school band. The 100-piece band sent the woodwinds home before the game, and the brass instruments froze up before the half. One trumpeter got his lips stuck on the mouthpiece. Moore, a 17-year-old high school student, wasn't identified for a week, despite a search for "the lone, frosted fan" by the college and the local media. He was eventually and rightfully honored at a Washington State basketball game and was reimbursed.

Twenty-two of the 28 residents of Joe, Montana (a.k.a. Ismay, Mont.) visit Joe Montana in Kansas City. Right: A sign welcoming visitors into town.

Photos courtesy of Loreen Nemitz

• The state of Montana is home to a whole town of football fans. Residents of Ismay, a farming community with a population of 28, voted in 1993 to rename itself Joe, Montana. The name change was unofficial and lasted only until the end of that football season. But the post office acknowledged the event with a special postmark in the shape of a football helmet. Many of the residents have even had the opportunity to meet the famous football player.

- What a difference a year makes. Before Northwestern won the Big Ten championship in 1995, the school had difficulty getting anyone to attend its home games. But in the spring of '96, school administrators announced that a block of 5,000 student seats, located in prime territory, would be relocated. They cited fans' complaints that the students stood for the entire game and blocked their view, but others claimed the university wanted the prime seats for alumni who showed renewed financial interest in the school. So, the students staged a one-week campus protest. The administration gave in and promised the students they could remain in their previous locations.
- Fans and former teammates of Iowa running back Nile Kinnick, the 1939 Heisman Trophy winner who died in 1943 when his Navy fighter plane crashed, attempted to find the wreckage in the Caribbean Sea in 1996. The group wanted to find the plane, salvage and refurbish it, then set it on a pole at Kinnick Stadium in Iowa City.

And then there are fans who are dedicated to hating a particular team...

- Sam Young was a stock boy for Minyard Food Stores in Dallas in 1996. When the company allowed its employees to wear Cowboys apparel during the club's playoff run, Young balked. A Washington Redskins fan at heart, but a backer of "anybody but Dallas," Young donned a Packers shirt the day the Cowboys faced Green Bay. When Young refused to change his shirt, he was fired.

Strike Up The Band

In college football, some of the biggest fans are in the marching bands. The most famous college band member to make an impact is Gary Tyrrell. He was the Stanford trombone player who was flattened in the end zone at the conclusion of the Cal-Stanford game in 1982. That day, Stanford kicked a field goal with four seconds left to take a 20-19 lead. There was only enough time remaining for the kickoff, so the Cardinal fans began to celebrate. Cal's Kevin Moen fielded the ensuing squib kick on the Golden Bears' 43-yard line. He lateraled the ball to Richard Rodgers at the Stanford 48, who lateraled to Dwight Garner at the 44-yard line. The clock ticked to 0:00 and the Stanford band began to take the field to celebrate. However, the play was still alive. Garner continued to run and lateraled back to Rodgers, who lateraled to Mariet Ford, who lateraled to Moen, who dodged fans and band members for the final 20 yards into the end zone where he plowed into Tyrrell. Says Tyrrell, now the controller for Orion Instruments in Menlo Park, Calif., and still a musician: "I was standing about nine yards into the end zone. I figured we won the game. I stopped briefly during the drum solo, turned around and I saw Kevin Moen a couple of yards from me and coming down pretty fast. And he knocked me on my butt. I figured he just wanted to leave the field because of the crowded mess. But I saw that he had the ball. That was pretty confusing. When I heard the cannon go off, I knew it was a bad thing." Says Moen, now living in San Pedro, Calif., selling commercial and residential real estate in Palos Verdes: "I didn't see him until I already ran over him. Even then, it was a blur. I was too emotionally involved in the moment of scoring to be concerned about who I was going to run over." Says Stanford coach Paul Wiggin: "That was the biggest fiasco of all time." And the trombone? It's being used as an FM radio antenna in Tyrrell's home.

That wasn't the first or final time the Stanford band was in the news. A 1988 performance titled "The Other Temptations of Christ" featured going through the express checkout lane with more than 10 items and using something other than a No. 2 pencil on a standardized test. At Notre Dame in 1988, the band formed a human eye and announced it was the Fighting Iris. Then it formed a fish with the line, "Win One for the Kipper." A whale was dubbed "The Humpback of Notre Dame." The band concluded its performance by slithering off the field in the shape of a lizard, "Newt Rockne." Through the years, it had shows dedicated to the kidnapping of Patty Hearst, phallic symbols, sperm and ovum, and condoms. The band traditionally ends its performances by dropping its shorts and mooning the crowd. In 1970 the mass moon wound up on national TV.

Stanford is not the only band to make headlines. Check out some of these musicians...

• Another college band famous for its outrageous acts is at Columbia. In 1988 at Harvard, the band made fun of native sons Sen. Edward Kennedy and Gov. Michael Dukakis. Band members first drove an imaginary car off a bridge labeled Chappaquiddick and then formed a set of bushy eyebrows. A year later, the band parodied the war on drugs, Sen. Jesse Helms' opposition to pornography and the proposed constitutional amendment prohibiting flag-burning — all in one show. Other show themes combined computer technology with safe sex warnings and the Christians thrown to the Lions (the day the Holy Cross Crusaders beat the Columbia Lions, 77-28).

• Other band members have also made a name for themselves. Tommy "The Toe" Walker is credited with composing the trumpet fanfare "Charge!" heard at games since the 1940s. But Walker was also the kicker for the Southern Cal football team. He would tear off his drum major uniform jacket, throw his baton to the ground and rush from the stands onto the field to kick extra points. He set a Pacific Coast Conference record for conversions in a season in 1947, then was hired as the band's director in 1948. He was named the first entertainment director at Disneyland. Later, he went into business as one of the world's leading creators of show business spectacles, including Super Bowl halftimes and Olympic opening and closing ceremonies. He died in 1986 at the age of 63.

• Gregory Allen Daniel of Shelby, Ohio, was a member of the Ohio State University Marching Band from 1971-73. What made him so unique? He was blind since birth.

• In Baltimore, a football band stuck together for 12 years, despite not having a team to march for. The Baltimore Colts Band was born in 1947, performing for all of the team's home games in the All-American Conference. In 1950, the original Colts departed. The band played on. Three years later, the NFL moved the Dallas Texans to Baltimore, and the local newspaper persuaded the team to rename itself the Colts. The 200-piece all-volunteer band performed for the fans until the

Photo courtesy of USC Sports Information

Tommy "The Toe" Walker pulled double duty as a member of the Southern Cal band and as a kicker for the football team.

Colts left the city in the middle of the night in 1984. Afterwards, local television station WMAR sponsored the band for five years until it could get on its feet financially. The band performed for the Baltimore Colts/Stallions of the Canadian Football League in 1995. When the Baltimore Ravens became an NFL franchise in 1996, the band cut a deal with the Ravens. The band will remain the Colts Band through the 1997 season. It then will retire on its 50th anniversary (and likely become the Ravens Band).

• But bands should be warned that too much of a good thing can be costly. The band from Cooper High School in Abilene, Tex., was sent a letter saying it owed $1,200 because its halftime show during a 1996 state playoff game in Texas Stadium was two minutes too long. According to the Stadium, fines can be levied because a long halftime show often causes a game to run long, which increases operating costs. Upon further review, stadium officials said the game didn't run long after all, and the band escaped paying the fee — this time.

• The Southern Methodist University band contributed to a loss by the school in 1986. During a game against Texas A&M, the SMU band was warned at halftime to stop playing music when the Aggies were calling signals. But the band played on. With the Aggies leading, 39-35, with 18 seconds left, the officials called an unsportsmanlike penalty on the band for playing too loudly while A&M had the ball. The 15-yard penalty gave the Aggies a crucial first down and enabled them to run out the clock.

The 12th Man

Tradition at Texas A&M calls for the entire student body to stand throughout every home game. The tradition started Jan. 2, 1922, when a number of Aggie players were injured during the first half of a game vs. Centre College. Student spectators were asked to join the team, just in case any more injuries occurred. E. King Gill volunteered, donned a uniform and stood on the sidelines for the rest of that game. Coach Jackie Sherrill took the students' involvement one step further in 1983 by organizing an all-student special team to cover the opening kickoffs at home games. In 1990, Rodney Blackshear of Texas Tech became the first foe to return a kickoff for a touchdown against A&M's "Twelfth Man."

• Speaking of the 12th Man, in an American Football League game in 1961, the Boston Patriots got help from a fan when it was least expected. On the final play of the game, with the Patriots ahead of the Dallas Texans, 28-21, Dallas quarterback Cotton Davidson threw the ball into the end zone toward a receiver. There was a throng of players, and a defender batted down the ball as time expired. The defender, though, wasn't a Patriot. A Boston fan had sneaked onto the field, run into the end zone and knocked down the pass. He ran off before the officials spotted him, and the play stood.

- A similar play decided the unofficial pro football championship of 1915. The Massillon Tigers, led by Knute Rockne, were at Canton to play the Bulldogs, featuring Jim Thorpe. Some of the overflow crowd was forced to stand in the end zones. Both teams agreed to a ground rule that said any player crossing the goal line into the crowd must have possession of the ball when he emerged from the crowd. With Canton ahead, 6-0, Massillon scored what appeared to be the tying touchdown. But when the ball carrier raced across the goal line, he disappeared into the crowd. The ball was knocked out of his hands and recovered by a Canton player. The runner insisted that a policeman had batted the ball away from him. "I know it was a policeman," The player said. "I saw the brass buttons on his coat." The referee, aware of the ground rule, called the play a touchback and awarded the ball to Canton. The players and referee debated the play for 20 minutes. The crowd became restless and stormed the field. The fans refused to leave, so the officials called off the game with eight minutes remaining. But the officials did not declare a winner. Finally, the referees agreed to settle the dispute. Their decision was placed in a sealed envelope and was scheduled to be read at 30 minutes past midnight, giving them enough time to escape from town in case the fans weren't pleased with the ruling. The officials declared Canton a 6-0 winner, giving them a share of the title. It wasn't until 10 years later that the truth about the "policeman" surfaced. A conductor on a train revealed that he was clad in a brass-buttoned uniform and indeed was stationed in a corner of the end zone. "When the runner plunged across the goal line into the end zone crowd, he fell at my feet. So I promptly kicked the ball from his hands and it went right into the arms of (Canton's) Charley Smith." Why did the conductor do it? "Well, it was like this. I had $30 bet on that game, and at my salary, I couldn't afford to lose that much money."

Rivalries

Some of the fiercest rivalries in all of sport occur between colleges. At Lehigh-Lafayette football games, students at the two Pennsylvania schools just 15 miles apart absolutely hate each other. In 1959, a halftime student tug-of-war at the freshman game the day before the REAL game turned ugly and both goal posts, the scoreboard and two flagpoles were leveled. At the 1975 game, 300 students rushed onto the field during the game and tried to destroy the goal posts. And in 1991 at Lehigh, students and police battled on the field and off it, resulting in several dozen people being treated for injuries. Administrations from both schools informed the students (and their parents) that future misconduct would result in expulsion. Needless to say, the rowdiness has diminished.

 While almost every school has a rivalry, not all of them are as nasty as these:

- Colorado School of Mines and Colorado College have had a heated rivalry since 1899. Following a loss in 1916, Mines students went to the CC campus and dynamited the goal posts. Any CC student who wound up on the Mines campus during the week of the game had an "M" burned into their forehead with nitric acid. In 1920, both student bodies began snake dancing on the field at halftime. A skirmish ensued, followed by a bloody riot. In 1951, Mines students tore down a goal post at CC following an upset victory and hauled the parts to the offices of *The Denver Post*. The goal post was presented to the newspaper's sports editor who had incorrectly picked CC to win that day.
- In Florida, there is an intense rivalry between Florida, Florida State and Miami. In 1995, ii inc. set up a 900-number called "I Hate U." The line's taped message referred to many of each school's transgressions, then asked fans to get some revenge by voting for the school they most despised. Miami won/lost with 50 percent of the vote.

    After Florida beat Florida State in Tallahassee in 1982, Gator fans rushed onto the field to tear down the goal posts.

Seminole fans rushed onto the field to stop them. Twenty-five policemen were sent to the hospital with injuries suffered in the riot.

- When Ohio State clinched its Big Ten title in 1996, it was at Indiana's Memorial Stadium. OSU fans stormed Indiana's field, intent on ripping down the goal posts. The posts in the south end zone fell just as the game finished, but the IU players completely surrounded the north goal post. Despite repeated attempts by the rowdy crowd, the posts remained upright until the police could clear the stadium.

- Wisconsin fans had a similar idea about tearing down the goal posts following a road game in 1979. As a group of Wisconsin fans flattened a goal post at Michigan State, the Spartan fans looked on with bewilderment. Michigan State won the game, 55-2. However, the Wisconsin fans paraded around the field and kept chanting, "We scored first!"

- Fans at Sullivan Stadium in Foxboro, Mass., in 1985 didn't fare as well. To celebrate the New England Patriots' season-ending victory over the Cincinnati Bengals, fans tore down a metal goal post and carried part of it out the stadium. The section came in contact with a high-power line, and five men holding the post were hospitalized with severe burns.

Bad News Badgers

Fans are supposed to be ecstatic over their favorite team going to a bowl game. But Wisconsin fans might be excused if they aren't too thrilled about going to the Rose Bowl again. The last time the Badgers qualified for the Grand Daddy of them all was 1994. Thousands of fans bought packages that included travel, lodging and tickets. However, what a large group of those fans found out once it got to Pasadena was that tour organizers had failed to line up game tickets. The fans were left to haggle over prices with scalpers who had a field day with the Red and White clad clan. The Badger fans' troubles caused federal legislation to change. The government imposed regulations on the travel industry that stated no one can sell an entertainment tour package without first gaining access to all the elements of the trip, i.e., tickets.

71

But ticket problems weren't the only bumps in the road for the Badger fans. One of the bus charter companies hired to carry several hundred of them from the hotel to the airport failed to show up. The fans were forced to take a caravan of taxis to the airport. Then a plane of 137 faithful sat on their chartered Boeing 727 at Van Nuys Airport for nearly an hour and a half before it rolled away from the gate. But then two wheels plunged through the tarmac's asphalt, forcing everyone to deplane and sit around some more. They were housed temporarily in a hotel, fed and then bused to L.A. International Airport. The only good news for the fans was that the Badgers beat UCLA in the Rose Bowl, a game many of the fans watched on TV.

Two months earlier, some of those same Wisconsin fans made national attention by celebrating a key victory over Michigan. Many fans racing from their seats in Madison's Camp Randall Stadium formed an avalanche of humanity that rolled over two fences. A total of 73 people were injured, six of them critically.

Props

Aren't the Utes of the University of Utah named after Indians? If so, then why did their home games in 1987 feature thousands of duck calls, duck bills and parachutists dressed like ducks? Utah led the nation in passing yardage, thanks in part to an offensive formation dubbed "Daffy Duck." Three wide receivers lined up on one side of the field, six linemen on the other side, while the center and quarterback went to the middle of the field and lined up in the shotgun. The formation was used only a couple of dozen times all year, but the fans fell in love with it.

Those fans may have been a little daffy, but these fans were sticky:

• University of Michigan fans began a short-lived craze in 1989. An unknown fan who brought a bag of marshmallows to munch on during a game became bored and began tossing them at his friends. His friends threw 'em back. The next week enterprising students were selling marshmallows by the bushel basket. It caused such a disturbance that fans spent more time having a food fight than watching the game. The fad was passed on to fans at Central Michigan. When the sugary substance began melting on the artificial turf and causing a mess, school administrators threatened to evict anyone caught throwing a marshmallow. Meanwhile, alumni at Michigan were not pleased with the disturbances and marshmallows were added to the list of items banned from being taken into the stadium.

Chapter 5

Hockey

Riots That Rival Soccer

One of the biggest riots ever was instigated by irate hockey fans. It was St. Patrick's Day, 1955, in Montreal. Thousands of fans poured onto trendy Ste. Catherine Street West and proceeded to break shop windows, loot the stores, set fire to businesses and automobiles and cause a major riot. It took tear-gas bombs to quiet the crowd, but not until more than 40 people were arrested and more than $100,000 worth of damage was done. What was the reason for the disturbance? The Canadiens' star player, Maurice "The Rocket" Richard, had been suspended for the playoffs. During the final week of the regular season, the Canadiens were playing the Bruins in Boston Garden. Richard was KO'd by Bruins defenseman Hal Laycoe, opening a bloody cut on The Rocket's head. When Richard went after Laycoe, he was intercepted by linesman Cliff Thompson, a former Bruins defenseman himself. The two tussled on the ice. The following day, NHL President Clarence Campbell shocked everyone by announcing that Richard was suspended for the remainder of the regular season, as well as the playoffs. Campbell showed up in the Montreal Forum for the Canadiens' next home game. It wasn't long before one fan attempted to get to Campbell, intent on attacking him. When that strike failed, fans began pelting Campbell's box with debris. One fan struck the president in the head with a large tomato. A tear-gas bomb, its origin unknown, exploded, sending the fans to the exits. The game was stopped and forfeited to the visiting Detroit Red Wings. Campbell escaped harm, but the fans still were hungry for retribution. They formed a mob and proceeded down Ste. Catherine, leaving charred debris in its wake. Miraculously, no one was killed.

It took a plea from Richard to keep the crowd from follow-up riots. Fingers were pointed in every direction to determine who was at fault. In the end, the Canadiens, without The Rocket, lost in the Stanley Cup finals, 4 games to 3, to the Red Wings.

 There have been other riots, too. Just look at how passionate these hockey fans are about their sport...

- Another hockey riot took place in Vancouver, following the Canucks' loss to the New York Rangers in the 1994 Stanley Cup Finals. More than 200 people were injured and more than 50 arrested as fans rioted on the downtown streets. Ryan Michael Berntt, then 19, was seriously injured when police fired a plastic bullet at him, aiming for his chest. He was struck in the head and was in critical condition on life support. "I don't know what happened after that. I woke up in the hospital a month later. I was in diapers and my right side was screwed — I couldn't move my right arm," he said. Berntt served a year in jail for taking part in a riot, possession of a weapon (a screwdriver), obstructing a police officer and assaulting two police officers. He filed a civil suit against the city and six officers, claiming police were negligent for shooting him in the head.
- Hockey also has seen its share of violence in the arenas. One was when the Buffalo Sabres' Rob Ray pummeled an unruly fan who jumped onto the ice during a 1993 game, but one of the biggest was in Philadelphia in 1972. At the end of the second period, St. Louis Blues coach Al Arbour was walking off the ice while arguing with the referee. When Arbour and the ref reached the tunnel to leave the ice, a cup of beer was thrown on Arbour. The entire Blues team rushed to the scene. Three players climbed the railing and entered the stands. Defenseman

Bob Plager began swinging his stick at fans, while other Blues were swinging their fists. Philadelphia police swinging billy clubs eventually forced the players out of the stands. After a lengthy delay, the final period was played. With Arbour coaching in a T-shirt (his dress shirt was ripped off during the scuffle), the Blues scored two goals to win the game. (St. Louis didn't win again in Philadelphia for 20 years.) Afterwards, Arbour and three players were arrested, handcuffed and taken away in a paddy-wagon. They were detained until 3 a.m. No fans were arrested or seriously injured. All charges eventually were dropped.

• On Nov. 23, 1996, two assistant coaches and a player from the Calgary Flames were suspended for an altercation with fans. At 16:31 of the third period in the Flames' game against the Edmonton Oilers, an Oilers' fan poured food and drink over the head of Calgary assistant coach Guy Lapointe. Lapointe took a swing at the fan. Another assistant coach, Kevin Constantine, attempted to climb the glass to join the altercation. The Flames' left-winger, Sasha Lakovic, partially climbed the glass and was suspended for two games. The Oilers also were fined for having an inadequate security response to fan abuse.

It is possible to be passionate and non-violent. These hockey fans are a little more original in their expression...

• In San Jose, the Sharks' fans are affectionately known as Hammerheads. They have the longest current sellout streak in the NHL, despite the team's less than stellar won-loss record. The Hammerheads get the attention of opposing players and coaches through home-made signs. Among the signs spotted: During a game vs. Toronto, "It may be spring, but the Leafs blow," and "Hey Toronto, nice logo. A leaf??" During a game vs. the New York Islanders, "Kasparaitis can be cured in our lifetime." During a game vs. Detroit after Red Wings coach Scotty Bowman admitted getting lost in the arena and locked in a room, "Knock, knock. Who's there? It's Scotty Bowman!" And during most of their home games, there are supportive signs in Russian and Latvian in honor of the team's foreign players.

Photo courtesy of the Chicago Blackhawks/Photo by Ray Grabowski

Brandan Grinwis, Jack Piazza, Sean Kapp and Paul Bivans are a big hit with Blackhawk fans.

- In Chicago's cavernous United Center, four Blackhawks fans decided to make their own noise during the 1996-97 season. They pound drums at every home game. Sitting in the 300 Level, high above the ice at either end of the arena, the four fans — Paul Bivans, Jack Piazza, Brandan Grinwis and Sean Kapp — bang their drums to incite the crowd. All four are long-time Hawks fans and part-time professional musicians, so they do more than keep a beat. "It's been incredible," said Bivans. "Now if we don't play enough, we're afraid the fans will chop our heads off."

- The Blackhawks also were guilty of one of the biggest crimes in hockey history. They allowed the Stanley Cup to be stolen. During the 1962 finals, the Blackhawks proudly displayed the Cup (which they had won the year before) in the lobby of Chicago Stadium. Montreal Canadiens fan Ken Kilander opened the trophy case, took the Cup and walked toward the street before being apprehended. While being taken to jail, Kilander said, "I want to take it back to Montreal where it belongs!"

From Hats to Rats

First there were hats. Anytime a player scores three goals in a game (a "hat trick"), caps traditionally have flown onto the ice from every corner of the stands. No one knows for certain when the tradition actually began in hockey, but the term most likely originated in cricket in 1882. It was used to describe a bowler's feat of taking three wickets on successive balls. The bowler's reward was a new hat. Some hockey clubs began to do likewise, and the practice of throwing hats onto the ice to celebrate continues today.

 If only hockey fans could have stopped at hats. You won't believe some of the things they've thrown since...

- In Detroit, fans began throwing octopus onto the ice during the 1952 Stanley Cup playoffs, and the tradition continues today. It was begun by Pete and Jerry Cusimano. Pete and his brother, Jerry, were avid Red Wings fans. The team had won seven straight playoff games, and the pair sought an appropriate symbol of success. Their father was in the fish and poultry business. The two were helping their dad before leaving for the eighth game at the Detroit Olympia. It was Jerry who suggested they throw an octopus on the ice for good luck. After all, an octopus has eight legs, and the team was going for its eighth straight victory. So on Apr. 15, 1952, Jerry threw his first octopus onto the ice. It weighed about three pounds, was partially boiled to turn it a deep crimson and was quite sticky. After that, Pete himself threw an octopus onto the ice at least once in every Detroit playoff series for the next 15 years. Other fans picked up on the idea. In a playoff game against Montreal in 1978, no fewer than 43 octopus — several of them still alive — were heaved onto the ice. Canadiens coach Scotty Bowman donned a helmet to avoid getting hit on the head by the flying seafood.

79

- Florida Panthers fans improvised on the octopus and began throwing rats onto the ice during the 1996 NHL playoffs. The team's leading scorer, Scott Mellanby, revealed that he had killed a rat in the dressing room of Miami Arena, then went on to score two goals. To celebrate his "rat trick," fans began throwing rats and mice — live, dead and toys — onto the ice during the next home game. More than 800 rats were tossed onto the ice after one score during the playoffs.
- In response to the throwing of objects onto the ice, the NHL passed a new rule prior to the 1996-97 season. The league warned that a delay-of-game penalty could be leveled against the home team anytime the maintenance crew was dispatched to clean up a mess on the ice. The Panthers issued warnings in the local media, made public address announcements and flashed a giant sign on the arena scoreboard showing a rat with a line through it.
- Objects thrown onto the ice haven't been limited to NHL games. Fans of the hockey team at Hamilton College in Clinton, N.Y., have their own traditions. Among them: fans hurl tennis balls and oranges at the opposing goalie in celebration of the team's first home goal of every season. On Nov. 18, 1994, fans celebrated a quick goal by pelting the ice with the usual tennis balls and oranges. But in addition, the ice was littered with apples, melons, two live mice and an inflatable doll. Hamilton school president Eugene Tobin wasn't amused. He banned all spectators, except for the players' family members, from the next home game. Said Tobin: "Extreme antisocial acts warrant censure."

That's Some Wait

The hockey fans at Rensselaer Polytechnic Institute in Troy, N.Y., have their own way of supporting their team. On Mar. 30, 1985, RPI won the NCAA hockey championship. The very next morning two students — Bruce Carroll and Jamie York — formed a line to buy season tickets for the 1985-86 season, even though tickets weren't scheduled to go on sale until Sept. 25. Carroll, York and their fraternity brothers took turns maintaining their place in line for 179 days. (That broke the school's long-wait record of 33 days set in 1983 by a group of ROTC students.) They filled their time by studying, sitting in a wading pool and listening to a stereo system that was hooked up. Just before the box office opened, members of the RPI hockey team served breakfast to the students in line. They were joined by RPI president Daniel Berg. When the time finally came, the frat members bought 19 season tickets, the best in the house.

Chapter 6

Soccer

The Soccer War

No fans rival the intensity and patriotism of soccer fans. After all, what other sport was partially responsible for a war between two nations?

In the summer of 1969, El Salvador and Honduras were playing a three-game series for a World Cup berth. The Central American neighbors were feuding already, but following the series there was a full-scale military skirmish — dubbed the "Soccer War."

Honduras won the opening game at home, 1-0. Hondurans assaulted every Salvadorian trying to leave the stadium. El Salvador's fans got revenge the following week when they witnessed a 3-0 home win. The Salvadorians made life miserable for the Honduras fans. Meanwhile, some of the 300,000 Salvadorian immigrants who were living in Honduras were brutally attacked because of the game's outcome. Soccer officials sensed that tensions were too high between the countries to stage another game in either nation, so the third and deciding game was played in Mexico City. The countries broke off diplomatic relations prior to the game. Nearly 2,000 Mexican policemen patrolled the stadium as El Salvador won, 3-2.

Two weeks later, El Salvador invaded Honduras, penetrating 45 miles with tanks. An intense battle raged for several days. For another month skirmishes broke out along the border. In the end, thousands of soldiers and civilians were dead.

 But some soccer fans have made news without being so violent...

- More than 2,000 fans in London staged a formal protest against their club team's poor play by walking out of the game with 15 minutes remaining.
- More than 15,000 whistles were passed out and used by Spanish fans to protest a questionable call from a previous game.
- A Romanian junior team, trailing 16-0, ran off the field with two minutes remaining in a game after fans threatened to strip all of them naked if they gave up two more goals. The club was fined 50 million lei ($14,500) for not finishing the game.
- Meanwhile, Italian fans who double as male striptease artists plan to form their own soccer team to raise money for charities. The team reportedly will play in standard soccer uniforms. "No loincloths. We prefer a classical uniform. After all, we are professional strip artists, not gigolos," said the team captain.
- The Red Tip Sexy Shop sponsors an amateur team in Mestre, Italy. The shop owner promised to entertain fans with porn stars and pompom girls on the sidelines.
- Enzio de Souza rode his motorbike 15,000 miles from Brazil to Los Angeles for the semifinals of the 1994 World Cup. The journey on his green and gold Yamaha 750 went through 10 countries and took 53 days.
- Fans in Brazil were barred from taking animals in the stadium after dozens took dogs and a tortoise to show their support for star player Edmundo, nicknamed "The Animal." "The place for native fauna is in the wild," said a government official.
- A British club warned fans that anyone caught entering the stadium with celery would be banned for life. Fans supporting the club pelted their overweight goalkeeper with the vegetable, a visual component of a bawdy song popular among British football fans for years. "The fans sang the song and then threw the celery up in the air. We estimate there must have been boxes of it in the air," said a club official.

The "Soccer War" might be the most glaring example of soccer fans' tragedies. Here, briefly, are others:

- In 1902, a grandstand in Glasgow, Scotland, collapsed, killing 25 spectators and injuring 517.
- In 1946, in England a containing wall in the stands fell open and crushed the spectators. A stampede killed 33 fans and injured 400.
- In 1950, Uruguay won the World Cup. Eight Uruguayans reportedly died of heart attacks as a result of the victory.
- In 1955, in Italy a referee was attacked by fans from Naples. When police stepped in, a riot erupted and 152 fans were injured.
- In 1958, five Brazilians were killed by gun fire during celebrations for Brazil's World Cup victory. One fan reportedly died of a heart attack while listening to the radio broadcast.
- In 1962, nine fans were killed and 30 injured in Gabon when a landslide hit the stadium during a game.
- In 1964, with two minutes left in a game at Lima between Peru and Argentina, two Peruvian fans attacked the referee over a questionable call. The referee suspended the game, causing fans to storm the field. When guards began firing tear gas, the crowd quickly turned and tried to exit the stadium, only to find the gates locked. Fans were crushed to death as the gates were forced open. The rioting continued in the streets. Three buildings and dozens of cars were torched, before the mob attempted to destroy the National Palace. When order was restored a day later, the body count showed 318 dead and more than 500 injured.
- In 1967, in Turkey 42 people were killed in a riot between rival fans from two teams.
- In 1968, 71 spectators died and more than 150 were injured in Buenos Aires. Celebrating fans threw burning paper from the stadium's upper deck, causing a rush to the exits in the lower level. The stampede crushed fans against closed gates.
- In 1970, when Brazil won the World Cup, two million fans began celebrating in the streets while awaiting the return of the

team. A total of 44 fans were killed and more than 1,800 injured in the mob.

- In 1971, as spectators were leaving a game early in Glasgow, a roar went up inside the stadium. Thinking their team had scored, thousands of fans reversed their direction and rushed back through the narrow gates to join in the celebration. A steel barrier collapsed, causing 66 deaths and 145 injuries.
- In 1974, in Egypt 49 fans were trampled to death when they stormed the gates to gain entry. Organizers sold 100,000 tickets for the game in a stadium that had 45,000 seats.
- In 1976, Omar Actis, the president of the Argentine World Cup Organizing Committee, was assassinated by left-wing guerrillas.
- In 1976, the President of Cameroon, who was watching an important match between his nation and Congo on television, called in paratroopers by helicopters to quash a riot that began with a referee's questionable call. Two fans were killed.
- In 1976, in Haiti a fan set off a firecracker, causing fans to rush for the exits. A soldier was knocked down, and his machine gun went off. Two children were killed. The rush to the exits caused a stampede; two fans were crushed to death and one spectator died jumping over a wall. The soldier committed suicide just outside the stadium.
- In 1977, 15 fans died celebrating San Paulo, Brazil's first league championship in 23 years. Eight died in crimes, five in traffic accidents and two with heart attacks.
- In 1981, in Germany three drunk fans celebrating a victory were thrown out of a bar. They let out their frustrations on a passer-by, beating him to death.
- In 1982, in Russia 340 spectators were crushed to death when fans tried to re-enter the stands after a last-minute goal.
- In 1984, in Italy a fan was stabbed to death while waving the flag of the visiting team.
- In 1984, British "hooligans" shot and killed a rival fan in Belgium.
- In 1985, "hooligans" attacked Italian fans. A total of 39 fans were killed and more than 100 injured.

- In 1985, fire engulfed the main stands of a stadium in England, killing 56 fans and injuring more than 200.
- In 1988, in Nepal 90 spectators were killed when they rushed for cover from a hailstorm and stampeded to locked gates.
- In 1989, 99 fans were killed and 200 injured when the crowd was crushed against a barrier in England.
- In 1990, four fans died and 60 policemen were injured in the celebrations that followed West Germany's World Cup title. Meanwhile in England, fans upset with their country's loss to West Germany, caused riots that left three dead and hundreds injured.
- In 1991, in South Africa 40 spectators were killed after rival fans caused a crowd surge.
- In 1991, Chile fans celebrating a South American championship caused riots that left 10 people dead and 128 injured.
- In 1991, one fan was killed and 24 hurt in Kenya when fans stormed the stadium gates to gain free entry.
- In 1992, 17 fans were killed in Corsica when a grandstand collapsed.
- In 1992, two fans were killed and about 80 injured in Brazil when a stadium's retaining fence collapsed.
- In 1994, a Brazilian fan was murdered by his brother-in-law because he praised the Italian team during the World Cup final.
- In 1994, a Colombian fan, distraught over his team's loss to the U.S., killed Andres Escobar, the player who was responsible for giving up the winning goal.
- In 1995, a spectator in Italy was stabbed to death by a fan from a rival club.
- In 1995, in France a spectator was shot to death during a clash of rival fans at a match in suburban Paris.
- In 1995, in Portugal two fans were killed and 27 injured when a railing in the upper deck gave way. Fans rushed to the railing to see the arrival of the team bus.
- In 1996, in Guatemala 84 spectators were killed and 127 injured when one section in the stadium became so overcrowded it caused an avalanche of humanity.

Sports Fans Who Made Headlines

- In 1996, in Zambia nine fans were killed and 78 injured in a stampede.
- In 1996, a Portugal fan died after a rocket-type firecracker hit him in the stomach during a game.
- In 1996, a 17-year-old Turkish fan shot and killed his friend while celebrating Turkey's first goal in a World Cup qualifier. In an accident a month earlier, an 11-year-old Turkish fan shot and killed his 13-year-old sister while celebrating a Turkey win. Prior to that, a 12-year-old Turkish boy hanged himself because he was despondent over a loss by his favorite club team. And finally, Turkish fans' random celebratory gun fire hit a 10-month-old baby in both feet.
- Other attempts at violence have been thwarted. In China, authorities come down hard on fans who cause a disturbance. Liu Guofang, who threw rocks that broke a window, was sentenced to two-and-a-half years in prison and fined 61 yuan ($22). Hua Zeping, who helped tip a taxi, was sent to prison for two years and fined 200 yuan. Two men were given four months in prison for throwing items and kicking a policeman, while more than 100 other fans were held in custody for up to three weeks for assisting in a riot.
- During the 1994 World Cup, about 200 people in Bangladesh smashed windows at two electric plants after a power failure cut off the telecast of the game between the U.S. and Switzerland. Two plant employees were injured in the attack.
- Also during the '94 Cup, Macoan coffee shop owner Lo Chon-yin collapsed and died while serving customers. He had stayed up two consecutive nights to watch games on TV after working all day.
- And bank robbers in Thailand took more than $40,000 from two safes when the guard left his post to watch a Cup game on TV.
- As organizers become more prepared in handling rival spectators, the fans become more sophisticated. Rival fans at a match in Germany, separated by increased security, used a cellular phone to set up a rumble at a local bar. The rioters broke windows, glasses, pool cues and bar stools. No serious injuries were reported.

AP/ Wide World Photos

Not even soccer great Pele has been immune to violence.

- Soccer fans showed an example of their loyalty when more than 6,000 sat in the rain in Portugal recently to watch the completion of a match that had been suspended because of a power outage. Fans observed two-and-a-half minutes of scoreless action; the game ended in a 1-1 tie.
- A fan in Brazil in 1973 showed that violence in the game has no boundaries when he fired a shot into the home of Pele, the greatest player of all time.
- The weapon of choice for unruly fans in Central America is urine. Beer-drinking fans in the stands fill empty cups with urine — saving them a trip to the restroom. Then they hurl the cups at rival fans.
- Soccer violence has become so acceptable in many parts of the world, that no one in Europe questioned the release of the video game, *Fever Pitch Soccer*. It features a segment re enacting Frenchman Eric Cantona kicking a British heckler.

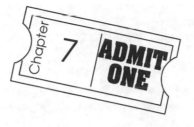

Tragedies

The worst tragedy in "sports" history occurred in Rome, Italy, during the reign of Antoninus Pius (A.D. 138-161). A total of 1,112 spectators were killed when the upper wooden tiers in the Circus Maximus collapsed during a gladiatorial combat.

In this century, the worst disaster was at the Hong Kong Jockey Club where 604 fans were killed when the stands collapsed and caught fire, Feb. 26, 1918.

The most publicized tragedy in recent times was the bombing in Atlanta's Centennial Olympic Park, July 27, 1996. A pipe bomb exploded, killing Olympics fan Alice Hawthorne of Albany, Ga., and injuring 111 others. Hawthorne was the co-owner of a hot dog and ice cream parlor, the mother of two and an active participant in community activities. Her funeral services were attended by President Bill Clinton.

The bomb exploded at 1:25 a.m. in the popular park that was packed with revelers and people watchers. Later, Melih Uzunyol, a cameraman for Turkish Television, died of a heart attack while covering the explosion.

Racing Deaths

At the Indianapolis 500, nine spectators have been killed. The most recent was in 1987 when Lyle Kurtenbach, a 41-year-old salesman from Rothschild, Wis., was struck in the head by a tire

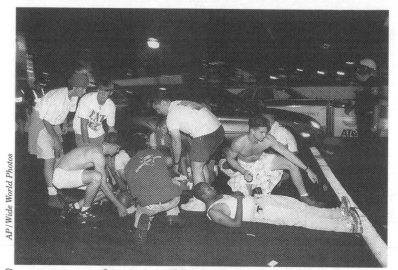

AP/Wide World Photos

Spectators tend to injured victims following an explosion at Centennial Park during the Olympic Games in Atlanta.

that came off a race car and flew over the track fence. He was standing in the top row of Stand K on the outside of the oval, about 50 feet higher than the track surface. The 18-pound wheel came off the car driven by Tony Bettenhausen and was rolling along the track. It was struck by Roberto Guerrero's car and flipped into the air between the third and fourth turns. Kurtenbach was attending his ninth 500 race and was sitting with a group of 10 relatives who had traveled from the upper Midwest.

- Two fans were killed at Indy in 1960 when their homemade scaffold collapsed in the infield in Turn 3. Fred Linder, 33, of Indianapolis, and William Craig, 37, of Zionsville, Ind., were crushed to death. Sixty-four other fans were injured.

- At the 1938 race, Everett Spence of Terre Haute, Ind., was struck by a wheel off Emil Andres' car; Bert Schoup, 16, of Lafayette, Ind., was killed in 1923 when he was struck by Tom Alley's car on a backstretch crash; and in 1909, Homer H. Joliff of Franklin, Ind., and James West of Indianapolis were hit and killed by a car during a crash.

- Two of the more unusual deaths at Indy were: In 1991, three days after the race, Stephen C. White, 31, of Indianapolis, illegally drove his truck onto the track while clean-up crews were on the grounds. When he wouldn't get off the track, security staff parked a van across the main straightaway as a road block. White plowed into the van and was killed. In 1931, 11-year-old Wilbur Brink III died of head injuries after he was hit by a tire that flew off Billy Arnold's car. Brink was not at the race, though. He was sitting in the front yard of his home on Georgetown Road, about 200 feet from the track's northwest turn.

 But Indy is no more dangerous than any other track. Here are other race-related deaths:

- Seven-year-old Lindsey Mayden, of Salem, Ind., died Oct. 17, 1996, after being struck in the back of the head by a bouncing tire while playing in the infield at Salem Speedway. Her father, Jeff Mayden, and uncle, Pete Mayden, both race at the track.
- Vickie Lynn Foster, 36, of Fredericksburg, Va., was killed at Sumerduck Raceway near Warrentown, Va., Nov. 10, 1996. She was hit when Daniel Ray George's car went out of control at a National Hot Rod Association event.
- Five people were killed when a car spun out of control and flew into a crowd of spectators at Alencon, France, July 14, 1996. Twenty-two others were injured when Belgian Jos Sterkens' car went into the stands at the Inter-Nations Cup.
- Belgian Ludo Briers, 45, was killed Aug. 23, 1996, at the 1,000 Lakes Rally in Jyvaskyla, Finland. A car driven by Dane Richardt Karsten slid off the road and plowed into a group of spectators standing 60 meters from the road. Twenty-eight other fans were injured. A year earlier at the same race, a woman was killed when she stepped in front of a car practicing on the course.
- Three fans were killed at the Bodatious Motor Sports Park in May, 1995, at the 20th Anniversary All-Star Nationals mud-bog races. A four-wheel-drive car jumped a metal guard rail, vaulted through the air and smashed into a crowd of spectators in Cartersville, Va.

- A fan was killed and four others injured when a hydroplane hit another speedboat and crashed into a spectator wharf at the Valleyfield (Canada) Regatta, in 1991. Driver Daniel Brossoit of Quebec also was killed during qualifications for the North American championship.
- And a 7-year-old boy was killed in a 1988 powerboat racing accident on the Allegheny River in Pittsburgh. A half-ton, 16-foot boat going 120 miles per hour, crashed during the Champion Spark Plug Grand Prix and went into a crowd of spectators. A lawsuit filed by 21 victims of the accident was settled out of court in 1991 for $3 million.

Baseball Fatalities

- On July 4, 1950, Bernard Doyle, 54, was shot and killed in the grandstand of the Polo Grounds prior to a New York Giants doubleheader. A single .22-caliber slug hit him in the head, just above the left temple. Police never did uncover a motive or the killer.
- In the 1920s, Yankee Stadium was hit with a sudden rain storm, dousing all the fans in the right field bleachers. At that time, there was no upper deck in right field, and thousands of spectators rushed for the exits at the same time. As a result, two fans were crushed to death. One of the victims was carried into the Yankees' clubhouse where she died on the training table, in the midst of the terrified team.
- On Oct. 9, 1908, the New York Giants were hosting the Chicago Cubs in the season's finale that would decide the league champion. Thousands of fans without tickets climbed onto the stadium roof or perched on building ledges across the street. Others climbed the elevated train track. One fan fell to his death from the tracks. The newspaper account mentioned that once his position was vacant, another fan quickly filled the spot.
- In 1903, 12 fans were killed and 282 injured when an overhanging grandstand collapsed during a Phillies game at the Baker Bowl in Philadelphia.
- In 1938, John Warde was standing on the ledge of the 17th floor of the Gotham Hotel in New York, threatening to commit

suicide. The 25-year-old baseball fan stayed on the ledge for 11 hours while a live radio audience stayed tuned to the suspense. A friend arrived and tried to talk Warde down. "C'mon in, and let's go over to the ball game," the friend said. "The Dodgers are at Ebbets Field this afternoon." Warde responded, "I'd rather jump than watch those Dodgers." He jumped.

- Also in 1938, in Brooklyn, Robert Joyce was in a local pub disconsolate over another Dodgers' loss to the New York Giants. He was getting some good-natured ribbing from the fellow bar patrons. A shouting match ensued, and soon Joyce left. But three minutes later he was back in the bar, a gun in his hand. He shot one man in the head, another in the stomach. Both died.

- In July, 1969, the New York Mets were earning their title of "Amazing." They were hosting the Chicago Cubs in an afternoon game at Shea Stadium, and Frank Graddock was watching it on TV in his Queens apartment. Frank's wife, Margaret, wanted to watch the soap opera, *Dark Shadows*. Frank insisted that the lone TV stay tuned to the game. The couple argued, and Margaret was struck in the head and back. She retreated to the bedroom to nurse her injuries. After the game, Frank went to check on Margaret. She was dead. Frank was charged with first-degree murder.

- While Hank Aaron chased after Babe Ruth's career home run record in 1974, the entire nation watched. Well, almost everyone. A Florida cab driver died after shooting himself, because his wife forced him to turn off the TV and go to work moments before the dramatic record blast.

- According to documents at the Baseball Hall of Fame, in a California semi-pro league in 1899, a game was about to begin. All the players were there, an umpire was there, and there were plenty of fans. But there was no scorekeeper. One of the fans volunteered, and he was moved to a better location directly behind home plate. In the 4th inning, his pencil broke, so he borrowed a knife from a fan sitting near him. With his eyes focused on the pencil, he began to sharpen it. The batter hit a foul ball that struck the scorekeeper's hand, and the knife he was holding went through his heart and killed him.

Photo courtesy of Purdue Alumni Association

Purdue's Memorial Gymnasium honors the football fan and team members who were killed in a train wreck.

Football Tragedies

- Purdue University fan Newton Howard, of Lafayette, Ind., was killed when a 14-car train carrying the Boilermaker football team, band and fans — nearly 1,000 people in all — crashed into a coal train in 1903. A total of 16 people were killed — 13 players, a coach, a trainer and Howard. In the collision, the train's first car was halved. Riding in the second car, band members escaped serious injuries when the car left the track and went down an embankment. Purdue's Memorial Gymnasium is named in memory of those who died.

- In 1973, after the Denver Broncos lost to the Chicago Bears, 33-14, a fan tried to kill himself. He shot himself in the head, but the wound wasn't fatal. He left a note that declared, "I have been a Broncos fan since the Broncos were first organized and I can't take their fumbling anymore."

- In 1977 in Denver, a fan shot and killed one person and wounded two others at the Arabian Bar, because someone turned off the TV in the middle of the Broncos-Baltimore Colts game.

- In 1979, Raymond L. Wilson was turned away from a Super Bowl party at a Louisville, Ky., lounge. He returned with a .45-

caliber sub-machine gun and opened fire on the patrons. He killed one person and injured two others.

- Daniel Bulmahn, 52, of Tonawanda, N.Y., was killed Jan. 6, 1990, when he fell from the side of an escalator following an NFL playoff game at Cleveland Stadium. Bulmahn and several of his friends were on an escalator from the upper level of the stadium when he apparently stumbled and fell over the side, 18 to 25 feet, onto another fan. "There's absolutely no indication of any horseplay or fight," said a policeman on the scene. "It was purely an accident."
- Sang Pillon, 51, of Pampa, Texas, died Oct. 4, 1996, from head injuries after being struck from behind by a parachutist dropping in for a high school's homecoming game ceremonies in Spearman, Tex. The parachutist lost control during his descent and "came in at a 45-degree angle and hit with quite a bit of force," according to the Spearman superintendent.

Other Sports Fans Killed

- Brian Watkins, a 22-year-old tennis fan from Provo, Utah, was in New York to watch the 1990 U.S. Open. His family attended the tourney nearly every year. He, along with his brother, sister-in-law and parents, was waiting for a subway train at about 10 p.m. in midtown Manhattan after a day at the stadium. A gang of youths approached. One stabbed Watkins' father and robbed him of $200 at knife point, and one punched Watkins' mother in the mouth. Watkins was fatally stabbed in the stomach when he intervened, police said.
- Lightning killed golf fans at the U.S. Open and PGA Championship less than two months apart in 1991. On June 13, Bill Fadell, 27, of Spring Park, Minn., was at the U.S. Open at Hazeltine in Chaska, Minn. He was in a group of fans trying to find shelter from a lightning storm. They were huddled under a 30-foot willow tree just to the left of the eleventh tee. A bolt hit, and 12 fans fell. Six got up, five were hospitalized and Fadell didn't move. According to a witness, Fadell's hands still were in his pockets while paramedics tried to revive him.

    Then on Aug. 8, Thomas A. Weaver, of Fishers, Ind., was struck while he was leaving the Crooked Stick Golf Club in

Carmel, Ind. He heard the warning signals and attempted to reach his car. According to witnesses, "He was carrying an umbrella, and the lightning went right through it. He was right by the car and the doors were being opened."

- Six fans were trampled to death prior to a cricket match in Calcutta in 1968. Fans were fighting for tickets to see India vs. Australia when the stampede occurred.
- Howard Gomes, 42, died Nov. 10, 1996, after being shot in the chest in Colorado Springs. He was trying to keep his son, Keith Lewis, 21, from starting a fight after Mike Tyson lost his heavyweight boxing title.
- An 8-year-old girl was killed and 200 fans injured Dec. 25, 1996, when an overcrowded grandstand collapsed during a rodeo in Jalisco, Mexico.
- A retired principal of Buena High School in Ventura, Calif., died in the school gymnasium bleachers while watching a basketball game. Arleigh McConnell, 76, suffered a fatal heart attack Mar. 7, 1996, during the final minutes of Buena's 52-46 girl's win in the state's regional tournament. He was the school's first principal in 1961; he retired in 1980, but remained a fan of the girl's basketball team. Fans carried McConnell's limp body down to floor level, and the game was stopped with 2:04 remaining. Paramedics worked on him for 22 minutes.

Chapter 8 ADMIT ONE

Legal Issues

Football

Jay Moyer recently retired after a 25-year career in the legal department of the National Football League. He saw nearly every lawsuit involving the league or its teams for several years as head of the department. Of all the ones that crossed his desk, which involving fans stood out?

"It was the mid-70s," said Moyer, "and the St. Louis Cardinals beat the Washington Redskins on a controversial call. It was a pass play and a replay clearly showed that the officials had erred in favor of the Cardinals. A group of Washington fans got together and sued the NFL to reverse the decision. The case was finally dismissed, but who knows, maybe that was part of the impetus that finally got the instant replay rule enacted.

"Then in the mid-80s," Moyer continued, "a travel agent based in New York City sold packages to the Super Bowl game in New Orleans. When the fans arrived in New Orleans, there were no tickets, so the fans sued the NFL. They said it was because we had failed to sell the travel agent the tickets.

"And finally, there were the bartenders in San Diego," said Moyer. "They sued the NFL because they didn't like the game being shown on television in their market. They contended that it was hurting their business."

One of the most publicized lawsuits involving the NFL actually was filed by a player. Miami Dolphin Bryan Cox entered Rich

Stadium in Buffalo to a chorus of boos, taunts and jeers. Included were death threats and racial slurs. So, Cox sued the league under Title VII of the Civil Rights Act of 1964. He wanted to "take some affirmative action to stop fans from subjecting black football players to racial abuse." Following the filing of the suit, the NFL sent a new policy to the teams requiring each club to eject any fan engaging in racial taunts or displaying profane signs. The case was eventually dropped.

NFL fans aren't alone when it comes to resorting to legal measures to resolve their differences with leagues, teams, players or themselves. Here are some more unique fan stories involving the legal system. (Since some settlements require both parties to remain mum, some of these stories do not include names or dollar amounts.)

• Four season ticket holders of the Philadelphia Eagles were so distraught during the 1974 season that they filed a breach of contract complaint against the team for being "inept, amateurish in effort, and falling below the level of professional football competence expected of a National Football League team." The season ticket holders demanded a cash refund on their tickets. The Eagles won that case.

• Season tickets for the Washington Redskins are hard to come by. In fact, there's a waiting list that might get you tickets in say, oh, 100 years or so. In 1987 a Virginia court heard the case of a mother who was suing her son so he would return the family's season tickets, which she claimed he had stolen. The son said he would serve time or pay a fine, rather than return the tickets. The mother let the son get out of jail-time when she agreed to let him use two of the family's five tickets.

• Two Indiana U.S. Congressmen/fans didn't want to sue the NFL. They just tried to get a law passed and avoid the judicial system all together. The Pittsburgh Steelers scored a controversial touchdown that helped them beat the Indianapolis Colts in the AFC Championship game. Andy Jacobs, Jr., and Dan Burton planned a bipartisan piece of legislation called "The What Really Happened Act of 1996." It sought to require instant replays for disputed calls in sporting events. So, didn't Congress have more important problems to deal with in '96? Not according to Jacobs. "When I first came to Congress we exempted private professional sports from anti-trust laws, and I don't recall them complaining then," he said. "I think the team that got the most real touchdowns ought to win the game. A win or loss is like property values. A victory is dollars and cents for a city, prestige, and that appears on the bottom line."

- The NFL's commissioner isn't the only football head who has to deal with legal issues. Two Pennsylvania fans sued the commissioner of their fantasy football league based in Philadelphia. Andrew DeDomenico, owner of TD Fantasy Sports, was accused of defrauding Michael J. Kman, Jr., and Robert F. Gruschow, of $250 each. The fans alleged that DeDomenico inserted a mysterious ringer into the standings that won each week. The winner failed to submit each week's roster of players until after the games were played. Once his roster was revealed to the rest of the league, he invariably picked the players with the week's best performances.

- And speaking of football heads, a Wisconsin sports fan and inventor is embroiled in legal controversy. Ralph Bruno says his company, Foamation, Inc., has the copyright for the popular Cheesehead hat, worn at sporting events throughout the state. Foamation alleged in Milwaukee federal court that Scofield Souvenir & Post Card Co. violated its copyright. According to the lawsuit, the Cheesehead "consists of a wearable sculpture in the form of a cheese wedge, typically molded from polyurethane foam." Scofield is marketing a Cheese Top, similar in design to the Cheesehead, but made of different material. Bruno is credited with creating the "hat," when he made a prototype at home and wore it to a Milwaukee Brewers game in 1987. Do you want proof that the Cheesehead has become part of American culture? The Smithsonian Institution has requested one to be displayed in its Washington museum.

Cheeseheads!

- Brian Barnard, a Utah civil rights attorney, asked his state in 1994 to recall the vanity license plate of a football fan that read "REDSKIN." In a letter to the state's Motor Vehicle Division, Barnard said the term "expresses contempt and ridicule for American Indians." Kathryn Jackson, the owner of the plate, is a state employee and a huge fan of the Washington Redskins. A check of the MVD records showed these other Indian vanity plates, including references to the University of Utah Utes: REDSKN, REDSKNS, RDSKIN, BRAVES, BRAVES1, INDIAN, UTEFAN, UTEGAL, UTELITE, UTERED, UTES, UTFAN and UTES1.
- Holly Atwood, an exhibitor at a Dallas sports fair, filed a lawsuit for $5 million against the Cowboys' Deion Sanders and the event's promoter, PFP Inc. Atwood paid $350 for a booth and felt cheated because players didn't appear as promised at "The World's Largest Players and Fans Party." Sanders was one of the few players who actually showed up, but stayed just briefly to sign autographs.
- James Sabatino, 18, of Boynton Beach, Fla., and his alleged accomplice, George LaGuerre, 26, of Miami, turned themselves into the authorities after stealing 262 Super Bowl tickets for the 1995 game. They allegedly sold the tickets for $1,000 each.
- A Notre Dame football fan filed a lawsuit against...a tattoo parlor? Yep. Dan O'Connor visited a tattoo parlor in Carlstadt, N.J., and spent $125 to have a drawing of the university's leprechaun mascot tattooed on his upper arm. When he took off the bandage, the inscription read, "Fighing Irish." O'Connor's attorney said it would cost about $700 for a laser procedure to remove the tattoo, not to mention the pain and suffering. The parlor offered to squeeze the "t" into "Fighing." Said O'Connor: "You're not talking about a dented car where you can get another one. You're talking about flesh."

Baseball

- In Philadelphia, a fan sued a real-life mascot and won. Felicia Glick, 33, of Harrisonburg, Va., was awarded $25,000 by a federal court after it ascertained that she was injured by the Phillie Phanatic. David Raymond — the Phanatic — accidentally kicked Glick in the back and shoved her head forward while clowning around in the stands. She still was being treated for pain in her back and neck and sought more than $1 million in damages.

- Hollye Minter was posing for a photograph after a 1994 Texas Rangers game at Arlington when she fell from the railing of the right field "Home Run Porch" and landed 35 feet below on empty lower-level seats. The 28-year-old broke her right arm, two ribs and bones in her neck. She sued the Rangers and the stadium architects, HKS Inc., alleging negligence. A police report said Minter was sitting on the rail at the time of the fall and that a security guard had ordered her off. She denied she was sitting on the rail. But since then, the team raised the railings 16 inches, in addition to posting 250 warning signs.

- A Chicago Cubs fan was enjoying himself at a game in the mid-'70s when television cameras focused on him and a lady friend. The only problem was that the lady friend was not his wife. The wife found out, and the fan did not receive a warm welcome upon his return from the stadium. The fan sued the Cubs and their television carrier for invasion of privacy. Because of that fan, most sporting tickets today carry fine print on the back that reads, "...This holder grants permission to the Participating Clubs and agents to utilize the holder's image or likeness in any live or recorded video display or other transmission or reproduction in whole or in part of the event to which this admits him..."

- In 1960 when San Francisco's Candlestick Park opened, a special radiant-heating system was devised to warm 20,000 fans in the wind-swept stadium. The system didn't work, so Bay area attorney Melvin Belli sued the Giants for the price of his season tickets, claiming breach of warranty. Belli told the jury that he had been assailed by "the bitterest winds this side of the Himalayas," and to be comfortable at Candlestick Park a fan would have to dress warmer than he might for a Siberian expedition. A $55,000 wind study was commissioned by the city and showed gusts at the stadium could reach 62 miles per hour.

- Another bizarre lawsuit involving a baseball fan occurred in the 1950s. In Lodi, N.J., David Sassano was making a purchase in a liquor store owned by Sam Graceffo. A TV set in the store was tuned to a New York Yankee game. After Mickey Mantle belted an extra-inning homer to clinch the American League pennant, Sassano celebrated by pounding his fists on a countertop. The vibrations caused a .32-caliber revolver on a shelf under the counter to fire, striking Sassano. Four months later, Sassano sued Graceffo for $50,000 in damages.

- But one of the earliest lawsuits involving a baseball fan took place in 1911. According to the Nov. 18, 1911 edition of *The Sporting Life*: "Whether a spectator at a base ball game has the right to call a player a 'stiff and a bonehead' will be determined in a $5,000 damage suit filed in district court by Erving R. Irving of Minneapolis against the St. Paul Base Ball Club. Erving and his wife were at Lexington Park to see the game with Milwaukee on July 8. He alleges he was put out of the grounds for criticizing Ralston, who was coaching for St. Paul players." There was no follow-up story to record the verdict.

- The Tiger Stadium Fan Club sued the state of Michigan to keep it from allocating $55 million to help in construction of a new Tiger Stadium in Detroit. The high courts said the Michigan Strategic Fund had the power to provide money without an act by the state legislature. The lawsuit was rejected following an election in which 81 percent of Detroit residents voted against reversing a city ordinance allowing the use of $40 million in city money for construction costs associated with the stadium. The Fan Club wants to preserve the existing stadium. "For less than the Tigers paid last year in player payroll," the club said in its newsletter, *Unobstructed Views*, "the Chicago Cubs renovated classic Wrigley Field."

- One baseball fan who did receive the mercy of the court was in Atlanta Traffic Court for ignoring a "Do Not Enter" sign on a street near Atlanta-Fulton County Stadium. It was when the hometown Braves were suffering through another losing season in 1987. The fan claimed he had attended 30 to 40 Braves games that year and hadn't seen the sign in question. His attorney produced another witness who testified that he hadn't seen the sign either when he accompanied the defendant. Judge Barry Zimmerman cut off the testimony of a third witness by saying, "Are you going to tell me you go to 30 Braves games a year, too? Is this going to be an insanity defense?" The judge dismissed the charges, figuring the defendant had suffered enough.

- Richard Lee Rubin was desperate to show his support for the local independent team. However, that support got the 18-year-old thrown in jail. Rubin allegedly robbed a bank in Duluth, Minn., in May, 1996. After the robbery, he stopped at the offices of the Duluth-Superior Dukes. "He walked in and picked out a jersey and a hat and set them on the counter, and said 'I hope I have enough to pay for it,'" said a Dukes clerk. "He reached down in his backpack and handed me a $100 bill." The clerk could see the rest of the cash in the backpack, and Rubin was arrested a few minutes later. It turned out he already was on supervised release for an earlier robbery of the same bank.

- Baseball fans in Detroit and San Diego called on the American Civil Liberties Union and the First Amendment to fight their battles in court. During the 1984 World Series, featuring the hometown Tigers, Miller Lite beer ran an ad campaign in which it divided a stadium crowd into one section yelling, "Tastes great!" and another section chanting, "Less filling." The Tigers' "bleacher creatures" soon improvised their own cheer: One group yelled, "Eat s---!" and another chanted, "F--- you!" Tigers officials spent two years trying to tone down the "creatures." The bleachers were temporarily closed, signs were posted forbidding chants and security guards were sent on chant patrol. The ACLU warned the Tigers that the measures constituted a "possible violation of free speech." When the Tigers changed the signs from "No chanting of any kind," to "No obscene chanting," the ACLU questioned management's right to decide what is obscene. Meanwhile, in San Diego, fans complained that their home-made stadium banners criticizing the franchise and its management were being confiscated. Enter the ACLU. As a result of discussions with the team, the ban on critical signs or banners was lifted. Similar bans were reversed in 1989 when the ACLU filed complaints against the Cincinnati Bengals and New York Yankees.

- San Diego fans also filed a class-action lawsuit, accusing the Padres of defrauding season ticket holders by trading star players like Gary Sheffield and Fred McGriff during the 1993 season. In the previous off-season, Padre President Dick Freeman sent letters to potential season ticket holders saying that the core of the Padres stars would form the team's nucleus for years to come. In the settlement, the plaintiffs agreed to accept a liberal refund policy for individual game and season tickets. In addition, the Padres donated 10,000 tickets to charity.

- Atlanta Braves fans also filed a class-action lawsuit in August, 1994, attempting to stop a players' strike. The fans claimed the Braves sold them tickets under false pretenses. The fans wanted a full refund on their season tickets, as well as $5 million in damages from the Braves, Major League Baseball and the Major League Players Association. A week later, New York-based Sports Fans Unlimited joined with Washington-based Consumer Federation of America to pressure Congress to put an end to baseball's "unregulated monopoly." Neither effort was successful in getting the players back on the field that season.

- Not even Little League baseball can avoid lawsuits. In 1995, 9-year-old Johnny Lupoli of Wallingford, Conn., was sued for $15,000 for hitting a spectator with an overthrow during pre-game warm-ups. The suit was filed by Carol LaRosa, who was hit in the jaw by the errant toss. Her injury required 60 stitches and left a one-inch scar.

- And finally in baseball, players may now think twice about tossing balls to fans in the stands. Philadelphia Phillies fans Diane and Paul Heath filed a $50,000 lawsuit against Terry Pendleton, the Atlanta Braves (whom Pendleton was playing for at the time), the Phillies, Veterans Stadium security, the National League and Major League Baseball. According to the Heaths, Pendleton flipped a ball to Diane three years ago. She dropped it, which caused another fan to jump over her seat to grab for the ball. In the process, Diane suffered "multiple bruises and contusions in and about the head, body, back and limbs; injury to the back and neck resulting in injury to muscles, nerves, disks, bones and ligaments." Said Pendleton: "It's just ridiculous. People who have seen me throw know I can't even hurt a little old lady anymore."

Tennis
• And tennis players might stop throwing balls and rackets into the stands, too. When Pete Sampras won the 1996 U.S. Open, he celebrated by tossing his racket into the crowd. He had done the same thing following his Wimbledon title. But this time his racket came down and blackened an eye of fan John Hopper, a 39-year-old executive with a New Jersey promotional advertising firm. Hopper asked for — and received — a public apology, and public restitution, for the "irresponsible act." Said Sampras: "I guess I'll never throw another racket into the crowd again. I apologize that Mr. Hopper got hit in the eye by my racket, and I'm willing to sign the racket for him in the hopes that he'll give it to a children's charity so it can be auctioned off and hopefully do some good. I'm sorry it happened, but I don't see where it makes me a bad guy."
• Another U.S. Open tennis fan would prefer to just be left alone. Jane Bronstein, a 54-year-old New York City native, sued late-night TV host David Letterman, saying he violated her right to privacy and left her with mental and physical pain from public ridicule. For weeks following the 1995 tournament, Letterman's show played a video-clip of Bronstein champing on a peach with juice drizzling down her chin. The footage aired at least six times. Once it was used as a punch line for his "Top 10 List," referring to Bronstein, a heavyset woman, as a "seductive temptress." Letterman also put a picture of the woman on a Times Square Sony Jumbotron with the caption, "IF THIS IS YOU...CALL NOW!"

Basketball
• Basketball has not escaped the courts either. In Indiana, a woman sued the Pacers, the National Basketball Association and Schick for an undisclosed amount. Schick had a promotional give-away in every NBA arena. Fans got a small shaving kit featuring a bag with the local team's logo and a few Schick products, including a disposable razor. Six months after re-

ceiving the kit, the woman used the razor to shave her legs. She cut herself and filed suit. Schick and the NBA no longer give away razors at games.

• Another mascot, "Burnie" of the Miami Heat, was sued by Yvonne Gil-Rebollo for $1 million after she claimed she was publicly humiliated and suffered severe mental and physical distress. At an Oct. 23, 1994, preseason game in Puerto Rico, Burnie — played by Wes Lockard — said he "just wanted to dance" with Gil-Rebollo. The woman countered that Lockard bruised her arm and broke her purse strap after he knocked her to the floor in front of 6,000 fans. The eight-woman jury awarded Gil-Rebollo $10,000 in damages.

• The University of Arizona is miffed at the state courts for what the judicial system has done with some of the prime seats to Wildcats basketball games. The courts have auctioned about 75 season tickets to help pay bankrupt fans' debts. The tickets have brought as much as $150,000 a pair, because most of the tickets belonged to members of the Wildcat Club, an exclusive group of big-dollar boosters. Traditionally, season ticket holders are allowed to renew their seats year after year, an expectation of the fans who purchased the auctioned ducats. Arizona prefers to re-assign those seats to other big donors to the athletic department, not to someone whose contributions were distributed to the bankrupt fans' creditors. The biggest problem, though, was finding a judge to hear the appeals. All of the local federal judges recused themselves from the case, apparently because — you guessed it — they were Arizona season ticket holders. A judge in Washington state was assigned to hear the appeals.

• If you thought Dennis Rodman's reported $200,000 settlement for kicking Minnesota courtside cameraman Eugene Amos was the first time the Bulls' forward was legally involved with courtside personnel, guess again. Rodman was hit with a $750,000 lawsuit for pinching an usher's butt during a Utah Jazz game in 1994. Lavon Ankers, an usher at Salt Lake City's Delta Center, accused Rodman (then a member of the San Antonio Spurs) of "willful and malicious conduct" that caused her to suffer "humiliation, shame, embarrassment and mental and emotional suffering all in an amount to be the subject of proof at trial." According to the suit, Ankers was working a court-side corner when Rodman ran out of bounds for a loose ball. "After regaining his balance, Rodman continued to walk away from the court and into (the area) where (Ankers) was standing. As defendant Rodman walked past the plaintiff, he placed his hand on the plaintiff's buttocks and pinched her."

Earlier, Rodman settled a dispute out of court for an undisclosed amount after Nancy Clark, a realtor from Indianapolis, claimed she lost two teeth when the forward collided with her while chasing a ball into the seats in Detroit's Silverdome in 1987. Rodman's attorney, Stuart Ulanoff, said in court that Clark would not have been hurt had she been paying attention to the game instead of rating which women in the stands were wearing the ugliest outfits. Clark's attor-

Rodman, shown here early in his pro career, has seen his fair share of legal problems.

Photo courtesy of the Detroit Pistons

ney, Michael Materna, rebutted by calling Rodman a showboat, claiming he shouldn't have tried to save the ball. Afterall, the Pistons were ahead by 35 points at the time.

- Chicago law firm Freeborn & Peters filed suit against LaSalle Northwest National Bank in 1996. The two companies share a luxury suite at Chicago's United Center, home of the Chicago Bulls and Blackhawks. The lawyers accused the bank of hogging the tickets for all of the good Bulls home games. The law firm claims it has suffered an "incalculable loss," since it can't entertain clients at important Bulls games. Officials at the bank claim the games were selected randomly. Lawyer Michael Freeborn said he arranged for a mathematician to testify that there was a "one in a gazillion" chance that the bank would pick the 11 best games randomly. But there was no debate between the two over Blackhawks tickets. Said Freeborn: "Michael Jordan doesn't play for the Blackhawks, does he?"

Others

- And Frank Barbaro, Jr., doesn't play for the Boston Bruins. However, that didn't stop the 22-year-old delivery man from Medford, Mass., from going onto the ice in the middle of a Bruins game. Barbaro was upset at referee Bill McCreary's failure to call a penalty against a player from the visiting team and jumped to the ice to argue with the official. Before Barbaro could get to McCreary, linesman Ron Asselstine checked the fan hard into the boards. Barbaro was removed from the ice and arrested, then announced his intentions of suing both the NHL and Asselstine. He claimed Asselstine used unjustified violence against him and caused him to injure his neck.

- In 1985 a New York family court judge wrestled with a decision on what to do with two teenage brothers who were overly engrossed in pro grapplers. He heard testimony from the boys' mother that the lads called themselves Hulk Hogan and Rowdy Roddy Piper. They smashed around the house throwing holds on each other and their mother, who had to avoid sleeper holds while she stood at the stove. Finally, the judge banned the family from watching any more wrestling on TV, or he would remove either the television set or the kids from the house.

- Some disabled fans have found the only way to enforce the Americans With Disabilities Act (ADA) is to seek relief from the courts. Deaf basketball fans filed a class-action lawsuit against the NBA and the San Antonio Spurs. The fans asked for captioning on big-screen televisions and smaller monitors already in basketball arenas. Captions would display game commentary, announcements and referee calls.
- Meanwhile, in 1996, the Justice Department sued Ellerbe Beckett, the nation's largest architectural firm, for designing indoor sports arenas in six cities that fail to provide disabled spectators with an unobstructed view. The lawsuit, filed in Minneapolis, charged that the arenas do not comply with the standards of the ADA. Finally, advocates for the disabled sued managers of the Oakland Coliseum, saying the stadium lacks legally required wheelchair access despite an expensive renovation. The suit claimed the wheelchair-accessible seats are confined to certain areas and are positioned so that their occupants can't see the field when someone in front of them stands up.

Memorabilia

The Babe Ruth of Memorabilia

Barry Halper is the Babe Ruth, Ty Cobb, Hank Aaron and Cy Young of sports memorabilia collectors. Here's a partial list of his baseball collection:

More than a million baseball cards (complete sets of every series of cards issued since the 1890s); nearly 1,000 players' uniforms; more than 3,000 autographed baseballs; every all-star game program; an autograph from every man, living or dead, in the Baseball Hall of Fame; the batting helmet Hank Aaron wore when he hit his record 715th home run; a set of World Series press pins for every game since 1911; a baseball autographed by Cy Young and the first 30 Cy Young Award winners; a sheet of paper with the signatures of every player who hit 500 or more career home runs; and Babe Ruth's uniform from his rookie season with the Boston Red Sox.

Halper, a father of three, runs a family business that distributes paper products and maintenance materials to stores, bakeries, restaurants and fast-food chains. He's also a limited partner in the New York Yankees.

He began collecting when he was eight years old in Newark, N.J. He collected game programs from the minor league Newark Bears, then had players autograph them. Newark player Lou "The Mad Russian" Novikoff gave Halper his first uniform — the road jersey that Barney McCosky wore with the Detroit Tigers in 1940. But he didn't begin collecting seriously until he was in his mid-30s. He attended a baseball card convention in 1974 and was hooked from that moment on.

Today, his collection is valued at more than $42 million. He claims to have more than $1 million in Babe Ruth uniforms alone. He keeps his collection in a three-room basement in his suburban New York City home.

So, what does he consider his best item? Lou Gehrig's autographed 1936 uniform. And what item does he covet the most? The uniform with the number 1/8 that midget Eddie Gaedel wore in his only plate appearance.

The sports memorabilia business continues to grow. The people who buy the items are among the biggest sports fans in the world. Some do it for investment opportunities, but most do it to be closer to the sports they love. Items no longer are just sold or traded at flea markets. Today the collectors who invest use the major auction houses of the world — Leland's, Sotheby's and Christies International. Recent items sold include:

- Tom Seaver's 1969 New York Mets uniform, $55,000.
- Don Mattingly's hair clippings, $3,000.
- Twenty-three golf clubs that belonged to Willie Park, Bobby Jones and other past British Open champions, $1,031,101.
- Lou Gehrig's 1927 New York Yankees road jersey, $363,000.
- Written agreement trading Babe Ruth to the Yankees, $99,000.
- Bat and ball from Pete Rose's record-breaking 4,192nd hit, $125,000.
- Jack Dempsey's heavyweight championship belt, $50,000.
- Mickey Mantle's childhood home in Oklahoma, $60,000.
- Mantle's 1952 Topps baseball card, $121,000.
- Former Sen. Bill Bradley's New York Knicks jersey, $15,000.

The Honus Grail

The most valuable single item is a 1910 Honus Wagner baseball card. There were only about 150 of the cards made and less than 50 of them still exists. Only six of them are in excellent condition. One of those sold in September, 1996, for $640,500. The buyer of the card wasn't identified, but the seller was Patricia Gibbs, a 41-year-old Post Office clerk from Hollywood, Fla. She won the card seven months earlier through a sweepstakes sponsored by Wal-Mart, but was forced to sell it when she found out the prize carried a tax bill of more than $150,000. In 1991, a collector from California sold the same card at auction for $451,000 to Wayne Gretzky and Bruce McNall, former owner of the Los Angeles Kings. Gretzky bought his partner's share in 1994, then sold the card for $500,000 to an Alabama company that joined Wal-Mart in the give-away.

 Here are some other pretty amazing finds that sports fans would die for...

- Leland's auction house in New York recently was contacted by a 90-year-old Maine woman. She claimed to have 48 autographs on a team photo of the 1927 New York Yankees. At first, Leland's was skeptical. "She told me that the signatures were obtained at the front desk of the Princess Martha Hotel in St. Petersburg, where the team trained in 1928," said Joshua Leland Evans. "As each player checked in, the clerk pulled out the picture and had them sign. I asked her how she knew they were authentic. She told me she was the clerk and pulled out a photo of herself at the front desk to prove it. That was good enough for me." It is valued between $15,000 and $20,000.
- Sports fans will collect almost anything. Look at Ron Schwinnen, a 59-year-old used-car salesman in Chicago. He collects sports-related cereal boxes. He owns more than 400 different designs. Most are Wheaties. Some are Kellogg's Frosted Flakes and Corn Flakes. "To my knowledge, there are none I don't have," Schwinnen claims. "If there was a box I didn't have, yes, I'd pay through the nose for it." The first athlete to appear on a cereal box was pole vaulter Bob Richards. He was selected from more than 500 candidates and adorned his first Wheaties box in 1956.

Stadium Souvenirs

One of the biggest crazes for collectors recently is memorabilia from stadiums:

- An auction of items from the Boston Garden brought in $505,195. The organ sold for about $1,000; the scoreboard went for $20,000; the Zamboni was $15,000 (bought by a local ice rink); Bruins star Cam Neely's mouthpiece fetched $550 (purchased by a local attorney); Red Auerbach's loge seat sold for $5,000; and the mop used to wipe the sweat off the floor — autographed by mopper Spider Edwards — went for $1,600 (bought by long-time Celtics season ticket holder Josh Wolfe).

Photo courtesy of the Boston Celtics

Would you pay $5000 for Red Auerbach's loge seat? One fan did.

- A total of 30 Notre Dame Stadium items reaped $27,027.
- Chicago's old Comiskey Park raised more than $800,000.
- Among the items sold in auction from Cleveland's Municipal Stadium was Bernie Kosar's locker ($2,000) and the commode from former Browns owner Art Modell's office ($2,700). Gary Bauer bought the commode so he could hang it from the ceiling in his Cleveland bar. Bench seats sold for $35 and a block of four wooden chairs went for $350.
- When Cincinnati's Crosley Field was being torn down in the 1960s, Larry Loebbers of Union, Ky., went to get two seats for his recreation room. "It was a cold day in January and nobody was there to buy the stuff, and, well, one thing just led to another," he said. Loebbers wound up buying both dugouts, the interior of both clubhouses, the foul poles, scoreboard, the bullpens, the left field wall, 400 grandstand seats, a ticket booth, a popcorn stand and all the Crosley Field signs.
- The Dallas Cowboys replaced the artificial turf in Texas Stadium prior to the 1996 season. The turf was originally installed in 1981, and the Cowboys won three Super Bowls in that period. Souvenirs ranged in price from $24.95 for a six-inch star of turf to $100,000 for an entire end zone.

Catch One For Yourself

Among the most magical of sports souvenirs is a ball caught in the stands of a Major League Baseball game. In 1904 the big leagues created a rule giving teams the option of retrieving balls hit into the stands. When Charles Weeghman bought the Chicago Cubs in 1916, all the major league teams required fans to return balls hit into the stands. For publicity, the Cubs began letting the fans keep foul balls. Over time, all of the other teams adopted the same policy, but not without a fight.

In 1921, New York Giants spectator Reuben Berman caught a foul ball, but instead of returning it to an usher, he tossed it back into a crowd of fans. Berman was given a refund on his ticket and removed from the stadium. He sued the Giants for $20,000 for mental and bodily distress. Berman won the jury trial, but was awarded only $100. Because of the trial, the Giants and other teams finally gave in and allowed the fans to keep the balls.

- C. Allyn Russell of Concord, Mass., recalls going to an exhibition game in Albany, N.Y., between the Yankees and Albany Senators. "A foul ball was hit into the crowd along the right-field line," he said. "After a frantic struggle for the souvenir, the ball finally wound up in the hands of an overjoyed little boy. A bully overpowered the boy and ripped the ball away from him. The crowd in the grandstand booed, whereupon Babe Ruth, observing the action, tore into the crowd, wrested the ball away from the bully, and then lifted the lad high in the crook of his arm. With 10,000 sets of eyes riveted upon him, the Babe presented the baseball to the star-struck kid. The crowd roared."

- Atlanta Braves shortstop Jeff Blauser was at a hospital being treated for a broken hand he suffered during a game. Seated next to him was a man receiving treatment for a dislocated finger. The man injured his finger while attempting to catch a foul ball hit by Blauser. "He didn't even get the ball," said Blauser, "but he got a free trip to the hospital." Blauser sent the fan an autographed baseball.

- Banker Ron Vachon was in Boston's Fenway Park, Sept. 4, 1990. The Oakland A's Rickey Henderson hit a foul ball that ricocheted off a luxury box to Vachon's seat. He reached for the ball, but it bounced off his wrist. In the same at bat, Henderson fouled another pitch off the roof of a luxury box and it caromed to Vachon again. He missed that one, too. "The first one was a tough one, but I blew it on the second one," said Vachon. "I couldn't believe I'd have another chance. I just stood there and bobbled it."

- Jim Wright, a Seattle Mariners fan, leaned over the Kingdome's right field wall Aug. 26, 1996, and snagged a ball hit by the Yankees' Edgar Martinez. The umpires ruled the play a double, saying the ball would have hit the wall if Wright hadn't leaned over. The same thing happened June 29, 1994. The Tigers' Mike Blowers hit a drive to right, and Wright snared that ball, too, in almost exactly the same spot. It also was ruled a double. Said Wright, "I think it was a home run. That's why I caught it. Feet on the ground, ball comes to you, you catch it. You think it's a home run."

- In the summer of 1991, Eli Ganias was a 28-year-old actor from Freehold, N.J. He had just caught a foul ball in Shea Stadium and thoughts raced through his head. "Why not open a restaurant? And why not call it 'The Guy Who Caught the Ball's Place?' The walls will be lined with photos of me making the catch, and the ball will sit on a velvet pillow in the foyer. Tourists will wander in and ask a waitress, 'Is the guy who caught the ball here?' 'No,' she'll answer. 'He only comes in on weekends.'" Since that day, Ganias has become somewhat of an expert on foul balls. He spends a lot of time observing fans who try to catch baseballs. "Have you ever seen a grown man in the stands with a glove on his hand? It's not a pretty sight...If a ball comes to you, that's great. If you have to fight or run for it, that's fine, too. But if you have to interfere with the game, knock the ball out of a fielder's glove, or scoop a live ball off the field, it's not a legitimate ball to catch. You must not change the course of events...I saw a guy in the stands holding a baby in his arms. The guy dropped the kid to catch a foul. It's a tough choice, but in that situation you've got to hang on to the kid and hope the gods will smile on you again in a later inning. He did catch that ball, but the baby started to cry and the crowd let him have it. Some things are just more important than foul balls." Like home run balls...

- Danny Jones, a 30-year-old sales director from Towson, Md., was in the right field bleachers at Camden Yards when he caught Eddie Murray's 500th career home run, Sept. 6, 1996. Murray wanted to put the ball in a display case for his daughter, so the Baltimore Orioles contacted Jones and offered him a collection of Murray memorabilia in exchange for the ball. However, Michael Lasky, head of the Psychic Friends Network and a former professional sports handicapper, took out an ad in *The (Baltimore) Sun* offering $500,000 for the ball. Jones took the money — $25,000 a year for 20 years. Lasky originally wanted to put the ball on display to promote a hotel he bought, but later he set up a telephone poll and asked fans to vote whether the ball should go to Baltimore's Babe Ruth Museum or the Baseball Hall of Fame. Fans chose to keep the ball in town, at the Babe Ruth Museum.

- Following the sale of the Murray ball, Maryland memorabilia trader Robert Urban sought $1 million for the home run ball hit by the Orioles' Cal Ripken the night he tied Lou Gehrig's consecutive games record. The investor bought the ball for $48,000. He hopes to convince Wal-Mart to ante up. In the meantime, Urban is displaying the ball at an Eldersburg, Md., store. The manager of the store, Bill Adler, said he is happy just displaying the ball for now.
- But the fan who got the home run ball Cal Ripken hit the night he broke Lou Gehrig's record just gave the ball to Ripken. Bryan Johnson, who caught the ball despite wearing a cast for a fractured thumb, was offered $5,000 for the ball before he even left his seat. But Johnson, 33, met Ripken after the game and handed over the ball. Ripken gave Johnson a bat inscribed, "Bryan, thank you very much for the ball. It means a lot to me. We both share the same memory. Home run on 9-6-95. Cal." Johnson said, "This is Cal's moment. I wanted him to have the ball."
- Jim Barracca, a hotel manager from Long Island, caught the home run ball hit by Atlanta Brave Andruw Jones in Game 1 of the 1996 World Series. Jones, at age 19 years, 6 months and 28 days, was the youngest player to hit a homer in World Series history. Collectors told Barracca the ball could fetch $50,000 to $100,000. He's torn between donating the ball to the Baseball Hall of Fame and selling the ball to finance his children's education. "I want the best education for my children, and Duke is $30,000 a year," he said. "It's tough. If it pays for my kids' college education, that's great. If it goes to the Hall of Fame, that's great."
- One of the most famous home run balls was Roger Maris' record 61st in 1961. While Maris was closing in on the milestone, Sacramento, Calif., restaurateur Sam Gordon had promised $5,000 and an expense-free trip out west to the fan who caught the ball. Officials of the 1962 Seattle World's Fair offered a vacation package to the fair in exchange for the ball. Fans jammed the right field bleachers on Oct. 1, all hoping to be in position to catch the ball should Maris connect that day. During batting practice, Sal Durante noticed all the hitters seemed to hit balls into Section 33. So, the 19-year-old truck driver

and mechanic from Brooklyn, sat with his fiancée in Seats 3 and 4 in Box 163D, Section 33. They were situated eight rows back of the right field wall and about 10 feet from the edge of the Yankees' bullpen. When Maris did strike No. 61, it landed in Section 33. Said Durante, "I saw that ball coming — round, white and beautiful. It wasn't flat or oval-shaped, like a ball that has a spin on it. That ball was hit clean and true." Durante snagged it with one hand. "I fell backward over my seat and landed in the one above me. Everybody charged me then. I could feel hands all over me. Somebody had me by the arm, another had me by the leg, and one guy grabbed me around the neck. My right elbow was bruised, but I never let go of that apple." Durante was whisked away to the Yankees clubhouse where he met Maris. Durante amazed everyone by proclaiming, "Rog, this is your ball. You hit it and it belongs to you and every baseball fan. It's going to the Hall of Fame." Maris, though, told Durante to get what he could for the ball. Sal received the $5,000 bounty on a TV program, and the Yankees threw in two season passes for the 1962 home games.

- Another Roger Maris home run ball was worth more than its weight in gold to a fan. Andy Strasberg, now director of marketing for the San Diego Padres, grew up in New York as one of the world's biggest Maris fans. Strasberg was such a big fan that Maris knew the youngster by name. While at college in Akron, Ohio, Strasberg and five friends drove to Pittsburgh in 1968 to see Maris play after he was traded to the St. Louis Cardinals. Strasberg sat in the right field bleachers, Row 9, Seat 9, since Maris' uniform number was 9. In the third inning Maris hit his first National League home run and Strasberg caught it. That fall, Strasberg made the trip from New York to St. Louis to see Maris play his final game. A reporter from *The Sporting News* asked Strasberg about his trip and later asked Maris about Strasberg. Roger replied, "Andy Strasberg was my most loyal fan."

- Hank Aaron's 755th — and final — home run ball is in the hands of Richard Arndt, and he's not giving it up. Arndt got the ball while he was working as a member of the Milwaukee Brewers' ground crew July 20, 1976. He was fired when he refused to give the ball to the Brewers. Today Arndt lives in Albuquerque and has The Ball stored in a safe deposit box. Arndt hopes to sell it someday, preferably to someone who would return it to Aaron or donate it to the Baseball Hall of Fame. Said Arndt, "I'm not prepared to give it to Hank at this point." Said Aaron, "Legally, I think it belongs to me. I think he's trying to hold me hostage."

• Ralph Gay retrieved George Brett's 300th career home run as it rolled around the right field bleachers in Cleveland. The 55-year-old fan is blind and was on an outing from a local veterans hospital.

• The longest home run hit by Ted Williams in Fenway Park is marked by a red seat in the otherwise blue right field bleachers. It was June 9, 1946. Williams crushed a Fred Hutchinson fast ball and sent it deep into the stands. Joseph A. Boucher, a 56-year-old construction worker, was sitting in the 33rd row when the blast broke through his straw hat and clanked off the top of his head. "I didn't even get the ball," Boucher said. "They say it bounced a dozen rows higher, but after it hit my head, I was no longer interested."

• The New York Mets' Alex Ochoa hit his first career home run in 1996 at Philadelphia's Veterans Stadium. It landed squarely on the head of a spectator. When asked if he wanted anything in return if he gave Ochoa the ball, the fan replied, "Yeah, I want an Ochoa bat — and a bag of ice!"

"You can catch a baseball, you can catch a puck. But when it comes to football, you're out of luck." That was the rallying cry of the National Fan Alliance in 1989 when it appealed to the NFL to take down the protective nets behind the goal posts that keep footballs from going into the stands. Said an NFL spokesman, "If you kick a ball into the stands, you'd have people fighting all over. I see no way that we'd give into their wishes." Counters Steven David, founder of the NFA, "They say they're looking out for our safety — as they sell 20-ounce cups of beer to 50,000 people at 14 cities around the country and then put them on the freeway."

Chapter 10

Family

Whether it's Dad behind the backstop riding the umpire in his son's Little League game or Mom in Texas hiring a hit-man to knock off a rival cheerleader's mother, an athlete's family can be their best — or worst — fans.

Skating Turns Violent

Consider Tonya Harding. She was competing for the crown of women's U.S. national figure skating champion. But Nancy Kerrigan was one skater who could get in the way. At Detroit in 1994, Harding's ex-husband, Jeff Gillooly, her bodyguard, Shawn Eckardt, along with Shane Stant and Derrick Smith, planned an attack, then whacked Kerrigan on the knee, putting her out of the competition.

For their part, all four men spent time in jail. Harding was fined $100,000, made a $50,000 donation to the Special Olympics and paid $10,000 in court

Tonya Harding in the center of a media storm.

AP / Wice World Photos

costs. She also was ordered to perform 500 hours of community service, undergo a psychiatric evaluation, spend three years under supervised probation and quit the U.S. Figure Skating Association.

 The Harding-Kerrigan saga might be the best known family story in recent times, but other relatives have been just as involved:

• Jeff Tarango was a 26-year-old from Manhattan Beach, Calif., the 79th best tennis player in the world. It was July 1, 1995. He was in the midst of his third round match at Wimbledon, the farthest he had advanced at the prestigious tournament in his career. He was facing German Alexander Mronz and lost the first set. He was down 1-2 in the second set when a line call went against him. It wasn't the first of the day. He considered bad calls the norm when he drew chair umpire Bruno Rebeuh. But that day he had seen enough. After the questionable call, Tarango called Rebeuh "the most corrupt official in the game." He bounced two balls high in the air and walked off the court, quitting his match. Tarango's wife of a year, Benedicte, was sitting in the stands as she always did for his matches. She had seen enough of the ump, too. She walked to his chair and slapped him...hard. Later she said, "He speaks French, I speak French. I just try to slap him once. I don't think it's bad. I think it's good." Tarango was fined $15,000 for his (and his wife's) outburst.

• The pro tennis circuit has another family member who became somewhat infamous. It's Jim Pierce, Mary Pierce's father. Mary maintained a Top 20 ranking for most of her illustrious career, despite her father's propensity for unruly behavior. His conduct became so bad that the Women's Tennis Association passed what is commonly referred to as "The Jim Pierce Rule." It provides for the fining or banishment of any member of a player's entourage guilty of unruly behavior. It got its first use at the French Open in 1993 when Pierce was banned from the stately grounds of the Roland Garros after creating a disturbance in the stands. Some of his other transgressions? In 1992 he slugged two spectators and later bragged about it. He decked another fan in 1993.

- Moms sometimes get in on the act, too. In October, 1996, Cynthia Holmes, the mother of a Loyola High School water polo player, pushed Harvard-Westlake coach Rich Corso into the pool at the end of the match in North Hollywood, Calif. The local police said misdemeanor battery charges were likely to be filed. Meanwhile, in Manchaug, Mass., Jodi Alger was arrested and charged with assault and battery after allegedly punching Trevor Havard at her son's soccer game. Havard told police Alger confronted him and accused him of urging his son's team to injure her son to get him out of the game. Alger pushed Havard, then began to walk away, turned and punched him in the mouth.

- Minna Wilson, the mother of boxer Tony Wilson, did her best to support her son, too. Tony was a pretty fair fighter, earning the title of British light heavyweight champion. But in a 1989 fight against Steve McCarthy in England, Wilson was taking a beating. Minna climbed into the ring, went up behind McCarthy and began clubbing him on the head with one of her wedge-heeled shoes. The referee interceded and temporarily stopped the fight. But Minna attempted to go after McCarthy again. Security guards removed her from the ring. When the referee told the boxers to resume fighting, McCarthy balked and left the ring, expecting to be declared the winner by disqualification. But Wilson was awarded the victory when McCarthy, bleeding from his head from the attack, refused to fight.

- And in 1995, wives of players from the Miami Dolphins were accused of beating up a woman at a San Diego hotel. Elizabeth Reyna Barrack claimed she was "assaulted, kicked, battered, struck, hit, punched, slapped, scratched and pummeled," after the San Diego Chargers beat the Dolphins in a playoff game. Barrack, a Chargers fan, had recognized the wives in a hotel restaurant and "began to deride" them. Among the women charged was Jacqueline Fryar, wife of wide receiver Irving Fryar, Shonda Ingram, wife of wide receiver Mark Ingram, LaTonia Cox, wife of linebacker Bryan Cox, Angel

Parmalee, wife of running back Bernie Parmalee, and Melanie Jackson, wife of tight end Keith Jackson. Barrack sought more than $100,000 for pain and suffering and $6,000 in medical expenses. The case was settled out of court.

• Roy Spencer was a 59-year-old blue-collar worker in northern British Columbia. His son, Brian, was a hockey player who was called up to the National Hockey League for the first time in 1970. Brian's debut with the Toronto Maple Leafs was scheduled to be televised that Saturday night as part of the "Hockey Night in Canada." But when Roy turned on his television set that night, something was wrong. Instead of Toronto against Chicago, the local station was carrying Vancouver vs. California. Roy checked the schedule. It was clear: Toronto vs. Chicago. The station had made a mistake. So, Roy got into his family car and drove 80 miles to the station's headquarters in Prince George, B.C. He stormed into the office, pulled a gun and ordered the news director to put his son's game on. One of the employees called for help, and soon the Royal Canadian Mounted Police were on the scene. Roy opened fire, wounding one policeman, before he was shot in the chest and killed.

OUCH!

• Lena Feller, mother of Hall of Fame pitcher Bob Feller, was being treated to a special Mother's Day in 1939. She journeyed to Chicago from her home in Van Meter, Ia., to see her son pitch for the Indians against the White Sox. She was one of 30,000 fans in Comiskey Park, but had excellent seats along the first base dugout so Bob could see her from the mound. In the third inning, White Sox pinch hitter Marvin Owen lined a Feller fast ball into the crowd. It smacked Lena in the face. The impact broke her glasses, and blood spewed from her face. Feller rushed to the stands and watched as she was led out of the stadium to a local hospital. Feller was shaken up, but finished the game, beating the Chisox, 9-4. When Bob got to the hospital following the game, he learned that Lena needed six stitches to close a deep cut just above her right eye. Her face was bruised and both eyes blackened. She stayed in the hospital for two days before returning to Iowa.

126

- San Francisco Giants pitcher Bryan Hickerson watched in horror as a foul ball hit into the stands smashed into his infant daughter's face. Bryan's wife, Jo Hickerson, was holding the eight-month-old child when Matt Williams of the Giants tipped the ball into the stands of Scottsdale (Ariz.) Stadium during a 1992 spring training game. Paramedics examined the child and determined she had a contusion.
- During the 1996 baseball playoffs, the wife of one of the owners of the St. Louis Cardinals was removed from the stands on a stretcher after she was hit on the neck by a foul ball and knocked unconscious. Kay Hanser, wife of Fred Hanser, had no permanent injuries.

Positive Role Models

- The 1996 baseball playoffs also brought the amazing story of Yankee manager Joe Torre's biggest fans — his brother, Frank, and sister, Sister Mary Marguerite, principal of the Nativity of the Blessed Virgin Mary Church school in Queens, New York. Joe's brother, Rocco, had died earlier in the year of a heart attack, and Frank waited in a New York hospital during the World Series for a heart transplant. A donor was found between Games 5 and 6, and surgery was performed immediately. With Frank watching the game on a TV in his hospital room and Sister Mary Marguerite cheering from the stands, Joe led his Yankees to the world championship. "You realize how important the World Series is when your brother gets a heart transplant," Joe said. "The game is not less important, but not as important as what he went through."
- Ida Buscaglia's son, Sal, is coach of the University of Buffalo women's basketball team. Ida became the "Mom away from home" for all the women on the team. But Ida suffered from kidney failure and was on dialysis. It was difficult, but she made it to all 14 home games during the 1995-96 season. The UB Royals won them all. She died following the season. As a tribute, the team wore her initials "IB" on their uniforms and dedicated the 1996-97 season to her. In addition, her usual seat, in the front row of the stands, right across from the UB bench, was marked with a plaque: "Ida Buscaglia, Royals' biggest fan."

• Jim Redmond is the father of Olympic track star Derek Redmond. The gentleman from Great Britain had traveled to Barcelona to see his son compete in the 400 meters of the 25th Olympiad. Although Derek wasn't expected to win the gold, he was given a better than even chance of winning a medal. He won both of his preliminary heats and on Aug. 3, 1992, took his place in lane five for the semi-finals. He got off to a quick start, but 150 meters into the race, he tore a hamstring in his right leg. He came to a dead stop while the other runners finished the race. He then began hobbling down the track. Suddenly, a man appeared on the track, hurrying to the injured runner. It was Jim. "The first thing Dad said as he put his arms around me was, 'Look, you don't have to do this.' And I told him, 'Yes, I do.' And he said, 'Well, if you're going to finish this race, we'll finish it together.'" Derek hobbled on one leg, helped by his father. The pair — now one — completed the lap and crossed the finish line. Jim passed his son to the nearby medics. But despite the defeat, the Redmonds have gone down as one of the most memorable and inspirational scenes in Olympic history.

AP/Wide World Photos

The Redmonds were an inspiration at Barcelona.

• Another proud father is Ted Bielawski. His son, Joey, was a promising young baseball player. The father and son used to share the dream of Joey someday playing for the local Boston Red Sox. But Joey was killed in an automobile accident in 1984 at the age of 18. Ted didn't want the memory of his son to disappear. It took him 12 years to complete, but in 1996, the Joseph T. Bielawski Sports Complex was dedicated at the Mary Immaculate Academy in New Britain, Conn. The Complex includes the best baseball and softball fields in the area, built under the supervision of Ted.

His Name Is My Name, Too

Even though they aren't blood relatives, there's a certain bonding that takes place among fans who share the same name with sports stars or have a resemblance to a star:

• Dave Wilson was a little-known quarterback at the University of Illinois in 1980 when he battled the NCAA and Big Ten Conference over his eligibility. He was given the OK to play, then was sidelined over a technicality. He got court approval to re-join the team, but the Big Ten came up with another technicality he had to fight. He continued to fight and credits his namesakes, the David Wilsons of the world, with giving him some inspiration at mid-season when he needed it most. A David Wilson living in Birch Run, Mich., read of Dave Wilson's trials and tribulations, and decided to unite all of the David Wilsons in the world in a show of support. The Wilson in Michigan penned a letter to Big Ten commissioner Wayne Duke and sent it to 50 other David Wilsons he could find in the phone directories of nearby cities. He asked them to circulate it to any and all David Wilsons they could find. By his estimation, David Wilson is the 10th most popular name in the U.S. Dave wound up playing in every game that season and threw for a then NCAA-record 621 yards in a game at Ohio State.

• Another fan who shares the same name as an NFL quarterback is Jim Harbaugh of Terre Haute, Ind. Although Harbaugh never has met the Indianapolis Colts quarterback of the same name, Terre Haute's Jim is his biggest fan. He's such a big fan that the 58-year-old maintenance mechanic has collected more than 1,500 pieces of Harbaugh memorabilia. He earned the title of Greatest Sports Fan in Indiana in a contest sponsored by Windsor Canadian. His prizes included a satellite dish and 12 months of free service.

- When Eric Davis was playing for the Cincinnati Reds, he found out about the plight of a young fan who shared the same name. The two-year-old Indiana boy had a bone-marrow disorder, and Davis sent $5,000 to help with his treatment.

 These fans don't have the same name as a sports star, but they are often mistaken for one...

- He doesn't share the same name, but Green Bay's Jim Oelstrom feels a kinship with Packers' coach Mike Holmgren. You see, Jim is a dead-ringer for Mike, so whenever the 49-year-old goes out in public, he's besieged with people wanting to chat with the 48-year-old Holmgren. Said Oelstrom, "It's fun. It's cute. It's funny, is what it is. Nobody's really bothered me. We have a light time of it. Up close, I bet we'd look much different. I personally think I've got less of a chin that he's got. I said it's all right as long as we win. If we start losing, then what will happen?"
- At the 1985 Citrus Bowl in Orlando, Dennis Anderson of Merritt Island, Fla., went to his seat in the end zone. The Bob Uecker look-alike was shown on the NBC telecast and fans began swarming to him for autographs. He claims he told everyone he wasn't really Uecker, but that didn't stop bowl officials from having him help The Chicken lead cheers or the *Orlando Sentinel* from running a photo of "ex-baseball player Bob Uecker." It wasn't until one of Anderson's brothers called the newspaper that it was discovered the impostor was really the owner of a local termite-control firm.

You Can't Choose Your Family
- California Angels manager Joe Maddon pleased the family and friends of outfielder Darin Erstad when he started the Jamestown, N.D., native in a 1996 game at Minnesota. More than 3,000 fans — 20 percent of the entire city — made the 5

1/2 hour drive to see Erstad play. Maddon claims it was an easy decision. "I'd have been dead meat in that state if I didn't play him. I could get one speeding ticket there and never be heard from again," he said.

- The mother of an Oregon State University football player supposedly called the school's publicity office after looking at the Oct. 5, 1996, entry on the team's schedule. She asked, "What school's initials are B-Y-E?"

- Players' wives made the news in the American League playoffs in 1996. Some wives of Texas Rangers players had journeyed to New York to watch their husbands play the Yankees. They were seated in a luxury suite owned by a friend of Rangers Bobby Witt and Dave Valle. But when Yankee owner George Steinbrenner found out, he had them banished from the suite and moved into the stands for Game 2. Said Steinbrenner: "They were standing and yelling and screaming for Texas. Now rooting for Texas isn't what I had a problem with. They were blocking people's view. I asked the guy whose box it is to have them sit down, and one of them wouldn't sit down."

Promotions

Million-Dollar Shots

No promotion has received the national attention of Don Calhoun's million-dollar shot at a 1993 Chicago Bulls game. The 23-year-old office supply store clerk from Bloomington, Ill., flung a basketball 79-feet from one free throw line through the hoop at the other end of the court. It was Calhoun's first Bulls game in three years; he caught the eye of and was selected by a Bulls staff member simply because he was wearing yellow suede hiking boots. During a third-quarter time out, Calhoun bounced the ball once, took three little hop-steps and heaved it like a baseball. Swish! "The ball seemed to be in slow motion," Calhoun said. "But I knew it was in the moment it left my hand."

The crowd erupted, and Calhoun exchanged high-fives with the Bulls' players. Later, though, the insurance company the shot's sponsors had hired balked when it learned Calhoun had played 11 games of college basketball within the last five years. He had played briefly at Triton Jr. College after his career at Bloomington High School. The Bulls, along with sponsors Coca-Cola and Lettuce Entertain You, have guaranteed his $50,000 a year for 20 years.

After appearances on *Entertainment Tonight*, *Today* and *Dateline NBC*, Calhoun quit his job at Reliable Office Superstore and joined the Harlem Globetrotters. "People have been great,"

Calhoun said. "I think people have really been happy for me, no envy or jealousy. I mean, it is kind of like Cinderella. You know, sports and comedy are the two places where all humans of all different races can come together and agree on something."

 Now nearly every major sporting event has a high dollar promotion:

- Don Mattingly of Evansville, Ind., (No, not the New York Yankees' Don Mattingly from Evansville, Ind.) made a 33-foot shot at the 1986 Continental Basketball Association (CBA) all-star game in Tampa to win $1 million — sort of. Mattingly, an insurance agent, won a $30,000 zero-coupon bond that reaches maturity in 40 years — in 2026 — but he can cash it in anytime for the current value. The Easy Street Shootout included regional winners from the 14 CBA cities. Each contestant got one shot, and whoever made the longest shot won the prize. After the first contestant banked in a shot from just behind the three-point line, the third person sank one from about a step beyond. The fourth contestant missed. Mattingly then hit his shot from straight on, almost the identical shot he hit to win the qualifying round in Evansville.
- But neither Calhoun nor Mattingly were the first fan to win a million bucks from a sports promotion. Baltimore Orioles fan Anne Sommers won $1 million in a contest when Gary Roenicke hit a grand slam home run against the New York Yankees in a 1984 game. The contest, sponsored by Equitable Bank, specified the exact inning that a specific player would hit a home run.
- At the 1996 Major League Baseball All-Star Game in Philadelphia, a fan won if any of the all-stars matched the record 485-foot home run Greg Luzinski hit in Veterans Stadium 24 years earlier. No player came close.
- At the 1996 Major League Baseball World Series, Carlton Gamble, a 23-year-old student from Brighton, Ala., was randomly selected from three million entries in the Gillette Strike Zone Challenge. He had to throw a baseball from the pitcher's mound to home plate (60-feet, 6-inches) into a 30-inch by 18-

inch target. Despite coaching from Hall of Famer Rollie Fingers, Gamble's toss hit the dirt in front of the plate. He still got $50,000.

- At the 1996 Skins Game in La Quinta, Calif., Kirk Bryson, a 64-year-old corrections officer from New York, was randomly selected from more than a million entries in the Gillette Putting Challenge. He had to make a 10-foot putt. He missed, but still got $50,000.

- At the 1996 USA-Trinidad & Tobago World Cup Soccer qualifying match, 10 fans were selected at random by Veryfine Products. They each had one kick from 25 yards with a regulation soccer ball at a 19-inch hole on a specially designed goal. No one won.

- At the NBA All-Star Weekend each of the last three years, fans have been randomly selected to try a three-point shot (22-feet). In 1995 at Phoenix, Mike Hoban of Cleveland missed, but was rewarded with $10,000 from then-sponsor Foot Locker. In 1996 at San Antonio, 17-year-old Demetrius Houston of Ft. Pierce, Fla., bounced his attempt off the backboard and also received a $10,000 consolation prize. And in 1997 at Cleveland, 49-year-old Floridian Jim Valente missed, but got $10,000 from American Express.

- Another big winner on the basketball court was Rob Carlson who won $50,000 by sinking a half-court shot at a Vancouver Grizzlies game in 1996. Carlson, 32, admitted he hadn't been on a basketball court in eight years, and has not gotten back on a court since he hit the shot. After getting his money, Carlson bought a Grizzlies' season ticket package, paid off his Acura Integra, took his girlfriend on a trip to New York and banked the rest.

- Cory Clouse, a University of Cincinnati engineering student from Cleveland, upstaged the start of the 1994 college basketball season by making a nationally televised half-court shot worth a college scholarship. ESPN offered a year of college tuition and room and board to a student who could make the shot as part of the network's "Midnight Madness." Announcer Dick Vitale offered to "throw in the books, baby." Clouse was selected at random from the 11,385 fans at Shoemaker Center. "I thought it was way short," said Clouse. "But it just kept on carrying. After the shot, I was nervous. It was like, 'What did I just do?'"

Dick Vitale threw in the books when Cory Clouse won a scholarship from ESPN.

- At a spring training baseball game in Phoenix in 1996, fan Charlie Kissinger won a $22,950 van when the Oakland A's Doug Saunders hit a pinch-hit grand slam home run. The promotion was sponsored by Denny's, home of the "Grand Slam" breakfast.

 But not every promotion has worked out the way a sponsor plans. Consider these fans' plights:

- Gus Hutchins drilled a three-point shot at a 1986 Indiana Pacers game and won 20,000 quarters ($5,000) from a local bank. His ticket stub was one of six selected at random, but it wasn't until after he hit the shot that he revealed he was a member of the University of Indianapolis basketball and track teams. Oh-oh. The Dayton, Ohio, native was forced to make a decision. Did he keep the money and forfeit his final season of NCAA eligibility, or did he pass on the prize and finish his college education? Hutchins took the money and ran.

- Jake Young was a high school senior in Midland, Texas, in 1986, when he attended a Texas Tech basketball game. His program number was one of two drawn for a half-court shooting contest sponsored by a local bank. Young swished the shot and won a week's interest on $1 million — $1,538.46. But Young was on campus as part of a football recruiting visit, and the NCAA wouldn't let him collect the prize money. It was considered an improper inducement. "The money didn't come from Tech, it came from a bank," said Young. "I figure, since I bought the program with my own money, I should be able to keep it."

- Brian Callery, a student at the University of New Hampshire, still was celebrating his $10,000 prize — for making a lay-up, free throw, three-pointer and half-court shot, all within 24 seconds — when he was told he was ineligible. The contest was held at every UNH game in 1996-97, and Callery had participated in the promotion at a game a month earlier. The company that insured the prize money stipulated that a contestant could enter just once, so the 22-year-old physical education major was disqualified. However, a week later the sponsor said it would award Callery the prize package anyway.

- Chris Jackson, a Texas Tech student, thought he won $25,000 in a Lubbock radio station's Kick for Cash promotion. But he didn't receive the money because he broke the rules of the contest. He was randomly selected in a drawing and signed a two-page waiver stating, among other things, that he had not played organized football within the last six years. But after he booted a 35-yard field goal during a quarter-break of the 1996 Texas Tech-Baylor game, the station's insurance carrier discovered in a background check that Jackson had played at Houston Stratford High School in 1991. "It's one of those things that seemed too good to be true," said Jackson, "and I guess it was." Said KRLB general manager Chuck Heinz, "He signed the document. We're sorry. We wanted to give the money away."

- Allen E. Adams was one of three fans chosen at random for a halftime kicking contest at a 1996 Pittsburgh Steelers game. The fans tried to kick field goals to win a free dinner or a round-trip airline ticket. Adams missed all three of his attempts. Police Sgt. John Kearney, working on the security staff at the game, recognized Adams' name when he heard it announced. Kearney called his office and verified that there was a warrant for Adams' arrest, stemming from charges of simple assault, making terrorist threats, disorderly conduct and public drunkenness. The officer allowed Adams to finish the contest, then put handcuffs on him later in the press box, where he was a guest of the team.

- In honor of the 35th anniversary of the Florida State League All-Star Game, the host Brevard County Manatees came up with a promotion that if a predetermined event occurred during a particular inning, a fan would win $35,000. For example, one inning's event was a team hitting for the cycle; another inning's event was a triple play. George Englehart was the lucky fan whose name was drawn for the sixth inning. If there was a steal of home plate, he won. With one out, Vero Beach Dodgers speedster Kevin Gibbs reached third base. East All-Stars manager Jon Debus had told Gibbs that if he got to third, he had the green light. West pitching coach Darold Knowles — knowing it was just an exhibition game — went to the mound to tell pitcher Eric Dinyar to go to a full wind-up. "We wanted to try to win the fan some money," said Dinyar. "I tried to put the pitch high and away, so he could slide under the tag." So, everyone was feeling generous. Everyone that is, except West catcher Adam Melhuse. Gibbs broke on the wind-up, but Dinyar's pitch was low. Melhuse easily tagged out the sliding Gibbs. "I had no idea what was going on," Melhuse said. "If I did, I'd have watched him slide in safely and let the fan win. Maybe if I'd done that I could have gotten a cut of it."

Wacky Baseball Stunts

Baseball teams long have been the biggest sports promoters. Here are some of the noteworthy promotions:

- Former baseball team owner Bill Veeck is regarded as the cleverest promoter in sports history. In 1948, Veeck owned the Cleveland Indians and granted a fan, Joe Early, his own night, simply because he asked. Early had complained in a letter to the editor of a local newspaper that teams were holding "days" for stars who didn't need the attention or gifts. He suggested teams have "days" for common fans, like himself. Veeck created "Good Old Joe Early Night" for the 26-year-old night watchman at an auto plant. More than 60,000 fans showed up. Veeck had orchids shipped from Hawaii (at a cost of $30,000) to give to the first 20,000 women. Then Veeck presented Early with a number of gag gifts — an outhouse, a cow, a calf, a horse and a Model-T car. But Veeck didn't want Early to go home angry, so he also presented him with a new convertible, a refrigerator, a washing machine, luggage, a watch, clothes and a stereo system. Said Early, "Never in my wildest dreams did I think this would happen. One thing is for certain. It never hurts to ask."

- A year later, Veeck was involved in another unscheduled promotion. Cleveland fan Charley Lupica climbed onto a platform at the top of a 20-foot flagpole on May 31, 1949. He vowed to stay on his four-foot-square perch until the Indians — who had won the World Series the year before — were American League champions again. On Sept. 25, 117 days later, Lupica climbed down after the Indians were eliminated from the pennant race. Veeck was so impressed with Lupica's commitment, that he awarded the fan a new car.

- Veeck orchestrated another promotion Aug. 24, 1951, when he owned the St. Louis Browns. Veeck let 1,115 fans "manage" the Browns for a day. Each fan was given a large sign with "YES" on one side and "NO" on the other side. They were instructed to flash one side or the other in response to queries by the Browns' coaches. Majority ruled. The real manager, Zack Taylor, was positioned in a rocking chair in a third-base box, smoking a pipe and wearing bedroom slippers. The fans helped select the starting line-up, then answered such strategy questions as: Shall we warm up a pitcher? Infield back? Run on the pitch? The fans had one runner caught stealing, but the opposing Athletics couldn't help seeing the signs. That proved to be the only "wrong" decision by the fans all day. The last-place Browns won the game, 5-3.

- A promotion Veeck would rather forget is his infamous Disco Demolition Night in Chicago's Comiskey Park, July 12, 1979. The promotion, sponsored by local radio station WLUP, started out as a good idea. Fans carrying a disco record were admitted for 98 cents. Those records were blown up and burned in center field by disc jockey Steve Dahl between games of a doubleheader. Some fans threw their discs — ala Frisbees — onto the field during the first game. Then thousands of fans poured onto the field just before the start of the second game and refused to leave. Ninety minutes, 39 arrests for disorderly conduct, a half-dozen injuries and a torn-up turf later, the second game between the White Sox and Detroit Tigers was declared a forfeit.

- The White Sox also came up with the perfect promotion for the dog days of summer. The club allowed 320 dogs and their owners to watch the Aug. 28, 1996, game in Comiskey Park. There were video clips from famous dog movies and TV shows, such as *Lassie* and *Rin Tin Tin*. Music from Three Dog Night and Elvis Presley's *Hound Dog* were played. There were dog acts, dog relay races, a dog parade, a Frisbee-catching show, a dog costume contest (won by Chopper, an 8-month-old miniature dachshund, dressed in a hot dog outfit with replica buns on either side and paper in the color of mustard, ketchup, relish and onions on his back), veterinary exams, grooming tips, a dog adoption service, a dog latrine featuring hydrants and a tree and free dog treats. Overall, it was a dog-gone good day.

- The Brooklyn Dodgers held a promotion in 1946 to get women in the stands. They offered a free pair of nylon hose — difficult to obtain in the post-World War II era — to the first 500 women on Ladies Day. Unfortunately, the deal was so good most of the stockings were collected by women who didn't even stay for the game.

- The first known Ladies Day occurred in Washington, D.C. in 1897. The Senators invited women to the game for free. Thousands of ladies took advantage of the offer, mostly to gawk at heartthrob George "Winnie" Mercer, the Senators' pitcher. Mercer was ejected by umpire Bill Carpenter for arguing a call in the fifth inning. The ladies were not pleased. But they still were ladies, so they waited until the end of the game to storm the field. They attacked Carpenter, knocked him to the ground and ripped his clothing. With the help of the players, he escaped to safety. The women diverted their ire and began destroying National Park. They tore out seats, smashed windows and broke doors before police could calm them.

- The Boston Red Sox invited hundreds of area golf caddies for free admission to "Caddie Day" in 1949. Halfway through the game, a couple of caddies threw golf balls at the Philadelphia Athletics' outfielders. Then nearly every caddie in the crowd unloaded a pocketful of balls at the opposing A's, forcing both teams to seek shelter in the dugouts. After 10 minutes, it looked as if a hailstorm had hit Fenway Park. Finally, the caddies ran out of balls, and the ground crew went out and picked up more than 1,000 golf balls.

- Dodger Stadium looked as if it had been hit by that same hailstorm Aug. 10, 1995. Three times during the game, fans, upset with the umpires, pelted the field with souvenir baseballs that the team gave away. After the third outburst, with one out in the ninth inning and St. Louis ahead, 2-1, the umpires forfeited the game to the Cardinals.

- Texas Rangers fans threw their free promotional baseballs on the field in a 1986 game. However, the fans were venting their frustrations not on the umpires, but the hometown Rangers. With Texas on its way to a 10-2 loss to the Milwaukee Brewers, fans pelted the players with hundreds of balls in the seventh inning. The ground crew picked up the balls, and the game continued. Said Rangers General Manager Tom Grieve, "At least it wasn't Bat Night."

- Pittsburgh Pirates fans, irate at watching the Montreal Expos' Roberto Kelly circle the bases on a comedy of errors, flooded the field with sticks they yanked off flags given away at the door as part of Flag Night. The tirade caused a 13-minute delay while the ground crew cleaned up the mess. Said Pirates coach Rich Donnelly, "I'm glad it wasn't Paperweight Night."

- Reggie Jackson used to brag that he was so terrific that someone should name a candy bar in his honor. In 1978, Standard Brands Confectionery Division came out with a "Reggie Bar," and the New York Yankees gave away 44,667 bars on Opening Night. Jackson hit a three-run homer in the first inning, and as he rounded the bases, he was showered with the candy. It took the ground crew nearly 15 minutes to pick up thousands of candy bars.

- The Yankees also put a unique twist to Fan Appreciation Day on Oct. 2, 1982. Dennis Denbeck, 32, and Joe Turnbull, 32, put brown paper bags on their heads to protest the Yankees' fifth-place finish. According to witnesses, the fans and their families had just completed singing "Take Me Out to the Ball Game" during the seventh-inning stretch when two security officers told Denbeck and Turnbull to remove their sacks. When the fans refused, one of the officers allegedly said, "You'll do anything we tell you," and took a swing at Denbeck. Police reinforcements arrived and triggered a small riot. Denbeck, who lost a front tooth in the incident, said the guards threatened to toss him over the railing and down the stairs. Turnbull said the guards pounded his head against a wall. The two fans were arrested on assault charges. A third fan, Ed Pietsch, 33, was charged with disorderly conduct and harassment.
- The Cleveland Indians staged the league's final "10-Cent Beer Night" June 4, 1974. The popular promotion, used in several stadiums, turned unruly in the ninth inning. With the Indians and Texas Rangers tied, 5-5, fans in the right field bleachers jumped onto the field and charged Rangers' right fielder Jeff Burroughs. When Burroughs fought back, both benches emptied, and the players were surrounded by hundreds of fans. Fights broke out and umpire Nestor Chylak was hit in the head. At that point, umpires forfeited the game to Texas.
- The Florida Marlins let a group of young fans run the entire organization for a day. On Aug. 8, 1994, as part of "Switch Day," the Marlins let 80 kids perform the duties of the Marlins' front office personnel in every job from p.a. announcer to president. "This is a full-blown effort to reach out to the fans and young people of the community," said the Marlins' Ben Creed. "The kids will learn what it takes to put on a major league game and hopefully have a great time being part of our team."

 Minor league baseball teams have also had some wacky promotions:

- Fans of the High Desert Mavericks of the California League actually beg to bark like a dog at home games. Between the time the stadium gates open and the beginning of the game, fans who buy a hot dog can sign their wrapper and enter a contest. One fan is designated "Dogperson" each night. That "lucky" fan is given a hot dog costume and headgear resembling "Goofy" and moved to box seats near the home dugout. Every time the Mavericks score a run, "Dogperson" must climb on the dugout and bark out the number of runs the Mavericks have scored. The fan also eats another hot dog for every run.
- The Palm Springs Suns planned a Clothing Optional Night for July 8, 1996. The promotion was sponsored by Terra Cotta Inn, a nude resort. The nudists were to be sequestered inside a large tent with a darkened security screen. However, the club called off the promotion at the last minute. "After thousands and thousands of phone calls, we just realized the stadium, which holds only 3,500 people, was not big enough to handle it," said Terra Cotta Inn's Tom Mulhall.
- A short time later, the Suns scheduled Priscilla, Queen of the Desert Night. The drag queen event was to feature a costume contest, parade and AIDS education booths. However, it was canceled after a public outcry.

NBA Stunts

The National Basketball Association has had a rash of hair promotions:

- At halftime of the Atlanta Hawks' 1984 season opener, the team offered free season tickets to anyone who would get a Mohawk haircut. A total of 14 fans took the plunge, leading Hawks publicity director Bill Needle to quip, "In a city of two million, you figure there'd be 14 nuts."
- Chris Shea, 27, shaved his head live on a local newscast in exchange for two courtside seats to an Indiana Pacers 1995 playoff game. Most of the Pacers shaved their heads prior to the postseason, and Indianapolis TV station WISH offered the tickets to any fan willing to match the style. "I'm satisfied with the look, although it feels a little weird right now," said Shea. "It was well worth it. If I had more hair, I'd do it for the next game."

- And in Vancouver, the Grizzlies offered two free tickets to their Jan. 7, 1996, game for any fan who got a flat-top similar to the team's center, Bryant "Big Country" Reeves. The Grizzlies had 25 hair stylists on hand for two hours. They went through 300 fans and had an additional 800 people in line when the promotion was halted. Two women who wanted flat-tops had their hair cuts delayed until they could be clipped at center court.

 The other sports haven't escaped without their share of promotional gaffes.

- The Washington Redskins thought it would be nice to pass out souvenir seat cushions at their 1991 playoff game against the Atlanta Falcons. However, when the Redskins scored a victory-clinching touchdown late in the game, all 55,000 fans celebrated by flinging cushions in the air. The jubilation lasted for several minutes as fans attempted to seek cover from the projectiles.
- The patrons in Big Boy's bar in Spooner, Wis., always look forward to the Green Bay Packers-Minnesota Vikings match-ups. Big Boy's has a lottery in which customers draw the name of a Minnesota player. If that player receives a bloody nose during the game or has to seek treatment from a trainer on the field, the contestant wins a free drink. If the player is helped off the field, the prize if five free drinks. If a stretcher is needed, the patron gets four hours of drinks on the house.
- But Big Boy's bar tab is nothing compared to what a Belgian brewery had on the line Aug. 23, 1996. At the Brussels Grand Prix track meet, the brewery offered a free glass of beer to every fan if a world record was set. Alas, no one in the world-class field set a record. Lucky for the brewery, since 40,000 spectators crammed into the stadium.
- The Montreal Canadien fans are some of the most traditional in the National Hockey League. But on Oct. 18, 1989, they went more than a little nutty, spurred on by radio station CKMF's $21,000 grand prize in an outrageous-stunt contest. In the first period a fan jumped onto the ice and slapped a puck past Calgary Flames goalie Mike Vernon with a minia-

ture hockey stick. In the second period, another fan ran around the ice with a banner that read "CKMF." In the third period, a guy in a devil costume started climbing over the boards, but referee Andy van Hellemond skated over and pushed him back into the stands. Then near the end of the game, two fans who had climbed to the rafters rappelled to the ice carrying a CKMF banner. No word on the winner, but Calgary coach Terry Crisp wasn't pleased. "Everyone needs a little humor," he said, "but, jeez, didn't it get a little ridiculous?"

• A fan who won a Phoenix radio station's outrageous stunt promotion walked away with two Super Bowl tickets in 1996. The unnamed fan drove up in a truck full of manure. He jumped into the manure and swam around before conducting interviews while still seated in it. When the crowd began chanting, "Do it again! Do it again!" he did two ostrich-like head-buried maneuvers to win the contest. Then he had someone drive him through the streets of Tempe while he waved from the pile of manure.

Celebrities

I Must Be In The Front Row

Jack Nicholson and Bob Uecker have reached such sports celebrity status that their names are synonymous with seat locations in sports venues.

Nicholson is a familiar sight in L.A.'s Great Western Forum, sitting in the front row, usually in sunglasses, cheering on the Lakers. A front-row VIP seat in any arena now is referred to in the business as a "Nicholson Seat."

Uecker's popularity rose when he was featured on Miller Lite beer commercials, sitting in the worst seats of a baseball stadium. Today those sections are appropriately called "Uecker Seats" at all box offices.

 Politicians long have been sports fans, too. The U.S. President traditionally throws out the first ball on Major League Baseball's opening day. The President usually calls national championship coaches and invites national championship teams to visit the White House.

- William Howard Taft was the first U.S. President to throw out the opening ball of a baseball game. He did it in 1910, after umpire Billy Evans walked over to the President's box and, on the spur of the moment, asked Taft if he would like to toss out the first ball. He gladly accepted. Woodrow Wilson was the first President to attend a World Series game, in 1915. But Herbert Hoover holds the record for most World Series attended, three (1929, '30 and '31).

- Franklin D. Roosevelt threw out the opening day ball eight times as the President. His toss in 1940 still is remembered. While FDR stood in his field-side box, the players from the Washington Senators and Boston Red Sox gathered on the field in front of the President. Roosevelt cocked his arm and threw it — right in the camera lens of *Washington Post* photographer Irving Scholossenberg.

- By the time Ronald Reagan was the President, the chief executive was required to go to the mound and toss the ball to a catcher behind home plate. In 1986 Reagan, who had portrayed Hall of Fame pitcher Grover Cleveland Alexander in the movie, *The Winning Team*, heaved his first pitch 10 feet over the head of Baltimore Orioles catcher Rick Dempsey. He asked for a second chance, and then threw a perfect strike. On an earlier trip to Baltimore's Memorial Stadium, Reagan ordered four $2 hot dogs from a vendor. The President, who had a degree in economics, attempted to pay for his dogs with a $5 bill.

- According to legend, President Taft was responsible for the tradition of the seventh inning stretch. During the opening day game of 1910, between the top and bottom of the seventh, Taft rose in his flag-draped box to stretch his limbs. Fans thought the President was leaving and stood out of respect. (However, many baseball historians claim the tradition was born much earlier.)

- Once he was out of office, former President Jimmy Carter became something of a regular at Atlanta Braves home games. He received a standing ovation from the crowd when he caught a foul ball Apr. 19, 1996. But he was roundly booed when he dropped a foul pop during the 1996 post-season.

- President Richard Nixon considered himself the nation's No. 1 sports fan. He was a back-up on his Whittier College football team and continued to follow all sports, especially football. As the Vice President, he began offering plays to his favorite team, the Washington Redskins. He continued to offer advice, even when he was elected President. During the 1971 NFL play-offs, he called Redskins coach George Allen and suggested he run a flanker reverse with Roy Jefferson. Allen ran the play on 2nd-and-6 from the eight yard line. The result was a 13-yard loss. Once the Redskins were eliminated, Nixon called Miami Dolphins coach Don Shula at 1 a.m. "I thought it was some idiot calling at that late hour," said Shula. Nixon suggested the Dolphins use wide receiver Paul Warfield on some simple down-and-in pass patterns. Miami used the play four times in the Super Bowl. The play resulted in three incomplete passes and an interception. The following season, after the Dolphins won the Super Bowl, Shula said, "I also want to thank the President for offering not to send in any more plays."

• President Bill Clinton was embroiled in some controversy when he clearly cheered for Arkansas in the 1994 NCAA men's basketball championship. Some observers thought he should remain neutral, but Clinton was proud to back his home-state school.

• But Clinton's favorite sport is golf. Every chance he gets, he's on the links. During the 1995 Bob Hope Classic, Clinton was joined by George Bush and Gerald Ford. The final scorecard showed Bush with a 92, Clinton at 93 and Ford at 100. What the scorecard didn't show was: Bush hit two spectators, Ford hit one, and Clinton didn't hit anything, except for a few trees.

• Former Vice President Spiro Agnew also liked to play golf. At a tournament in Palm Springs, Calif., in 1971, he teed off on the first hole and hit a 66-year-old spectator on the arm. The ball bounced off the man and hit his wife. Agnew's next shot careened off the ankle of another spectator, who had to be taken to the hospital. Agnew picked up on the hole, and his gallery was more attentive the rest of the round.

• But not all Presidents have been sports fans. According to reports, Red Grange was taken to the White House in 1925 in the midst of changing the face of professional football. Illinois Senator William McKinley arranged for Grange to meet President Calvin Coolidge. "Mr. President," said McKinley, "this is Red Grange of the Chicago Bears." Coolidge shook Grange's hand and said, quite seriously, "Nice to meet you, young man. I've always liked animal acts."

• Other politicians have gotten in trouble for being sports fans. In 1996, dozens of Colorado legislators accepted free season tickets to Colorado football games, costing the school thousands of dollars. According to records obtained by *The Rocky Mountain News*, the school gave two season tickets to 20 state senators and 34 state representatives, charging them only $21 in tax for tickets worth $200 each. The face value of the complimentary tickets totaled $22,400.

Hollywood Fans

Among Hollywood types, actor Charlie Sheen, star of the movie, *Major League*, is one of the biggest baseball fans. In 1996, he wanted to catch a home run ball without having to battle other fans. So, he spent $6,537.50 to purchase an entire section of 2,615 seats in the left field stands of Anaheim Stadium. But unfortunately, no home runs were hit that day.

Sheen also paid $93,500 in 1992 for the ball that rolled through the legs of Boston Red Sox first baseman Bill Buckner in the sixth game of the 1986 World Series. However, Buckner claims he was given the actual ball after the game, and that he has it stored away for safe keeping.

 While Sheen may be the biggest celebrity fan, he is certainly not alone. These stars have also been known to show up on the sidelines...

• *Baywatch* star Pamela Anderson Lee owes a trip to a sporting event for her success. In the summer of 1988, she was a 21-year-old fitness instructor who attended a B.C. Lions football game in Vancouver. She was wearing a Labatt's T-shirt, and between plays an in-house TV cameraman picked her out of a crowd of 50,000 fans and flashed a close-up of her onto the stadium video screen. The crowd went wild, and Labatt's soon was using her in promotions. A year later she was on the cover of *Playboy*. By 1992 she was playing the Tool Girl on *Home Improvement* before becoming a star on *Baywatch*.

- Even though Elizabeth Taylor wasn't discovered at a sporting event, she did make quite a spectacle of herself at a 1989 Dallas Cowboys game. Ms. Taylor was asked to preside over the pregame coin toss, as a guest of Cowboys owner Jerry Jones. NFL referee Pat Haggerty was so star-struck that he asked the actress to call the toss, instead of the captains of the visiting Washington Redskins. (She called "heads.")

- University of Iowa alumnus Tom Arnold was attending the 1992 Iowa-Miami game when he offered the fan sitting next to him $1,000 if he would run onto the field and tackle Miami's mascot. The fan did and was arrested by the security staff. Arnold not only made good on the $1,000, but an hour after the game, he was there to bail out the fan and covered all of his court costs.

- A celebrity who actually played a part in determining the outcome of a game is Spike Lee. The New York Knicks' No. 1 fan incited the Indiana Pacers' Reggie Miller during the 1994 NBA playoffs. Miller taunted Lee nearly every trip down the court in the final period and lit up the Knicks for 25 points. Afterward, the New York media and fans blamed Lee for motivating Miller.

- Rock and roll star John (Cougar) Mellencamp lives in Bloomington, Ind., home of the Indiana University Hoosiers. He regularly attends Indiana sporting events and recently donated $1.5 million to the school for building an indoor practice facility. "Athletics is a very important part of the image of IU, and I thought it would help the athletic department and the enrollment at the university," said Mellencamp. The school rewarded the singer by naming the building the John Mellencamp Pavilion.

- It takes a pretty important person to get a private show from the Harlem Globetrotters, but that's exactly what Pope Pius XII got on Aug. 1, 1951, at his Italian summer estate. The touring Globetrotters were performing in Rome when they were invited to an audience with the Pope. After the team presented the Pope with a basketball, he admitted that he never had seen a game. Owner Abe Sapperstein replied, "If you'll lend me that ball, we'll show you some!"

- George Plimpton became a celebrity because he was a sports fan. The *Sports Illustrated* writer made a career of participatory journalism and parlayed that into star status. During his career, he wrote about his experiences pitching against a National League all-star team, boxing light heavyweight champion Archie Moore, taking five snaps as the quarterback of the Detroit Lions, playing goalie for the Boston Bruins and pitching horseshoes with President-elect George Bush at Camp David.
- Another sports fan who wound up a celebrity was Dr. Joyce Brothers. She won the grand prize on the TV game show, *The $64,000 Question*. She correctly answered questions about prize fighting, then became one of the nation's most recognizable psychologists.
- And one final word of advice. If you are a waiter, and Mike Tyson enters your restaurant, make sure you get him seated at one of your tables. At a recent trip to Gund Arena to watch his hometown Cleveland Cavaliers, he tipped his courtside waitress $500 for bringing him a soft pretzel.

Bits and Bites

Questions

Question #1: So what fans really did the "Wave" first?

The answer depends on whom you talk to. According to some sources, it began, appropriately, on Halloween in 1981, at the University of Washington. Robb Weller, former host of *Entertainment Tonight* and a UW graduate, along with Bill Bissell, the band and rally squad director at the school, orchestrated the cheer at a Huskies football game. The pair motioned to the crowd and used the p.a. system at the same time to give instructions. The student cheering section had been doing a vertical "Wave" for several years before they attempted the full-circle "Wave" in '81. However, professional cheerleader "Krazy George" Henderson claims he invented the cheer and got national attention two weeks earlier in Oakland at an A's-California Angels baseball playoff game. He used his pointed finger to keep the crowd moving. "I got it going section by section. When it got around to a section that let it die, the other sections that were trained to do it all booed. Eventually, everybody got the idea," he said. It was a take-off on a cheer he led at Colorado Rockies hockey games.

Question #2: So what team has the best fans?

Teams in several sports claim to have the "best fans in America."

In the NBA, several clubs hung banners to emphasize those claims. However, *Sports Illustrated* conducted a poll, albeit an unscientific one, of league players to find out which city has the most knowledgeable fans. The results: New York was the choice of eight of the 16 players who voted. Boston finished second with three votes; Indianapolis, Los Angeles, Portland and Washington, D.C. each received one vote. Conversely, fans in Washington, D.C. and East Rutherford, N.J., were named the least knowledgeable by the same panel.

Photo courtesy of the Indiana Pacers

Teams often hang banners to honor fans.

Meanwhile, *Baseball Weekly* surveyed 249 major league baseball players to rate the fans. Baltimore was the No. 1 selection, followed by Cleveland and Denver. The worst? Pittsburgh and Montreal.

Question #3: Where is the best place to be a sports fan?

If you're looking for a particular time period, try Minneapolis-St. Paul from May, 1991, to April, 1992. During that stretch the Twin Cities hosted, in order, the Stanley Cup Finals, the U.S. Open golf tournament, Major League Baseball's World Series, Super Bowl XXVI and the NCAA men's basketball Final Four.

Question #4: What were the biggest and smallest crowds?

The answer varies, depending on the qualifiers. More than 10 million fans line the route of the annual Tour de France bicycle race. But the competition spans three weeks. For a one-day event, more than 2.5 million spectators view the annual New York City Marathon. For stadium events, the Indianapolis 500 doesn't release official attendance figures, but every year more than 300,000 seats are filled around the two-and-a-half mile oval track, and an additional 100,000 fans party in the infield.

In the Olympics, the largest crowd for a Summer Games event is an estimated 500,000 for the 1964 marathon in Tokyo; for the Winter Games, 104,102 watched the 1952 ski jump near Oslo.

The record crowd for a soccer game is 199,854 in Rio de Janeiro to watch Brazil play Uruguay in the 1950 World Cup Finals. In boxing, 135,132 non-paying fans witnessed Tony Zale vs. Billy Pryor at Milwaukee's Juneau Park in 1941. The record paid crowd in boxing is 132,274 in Mexico City in 1993 to watch four title fights. The biggest indoor fight crowd is 63,350 at New Orleans' Superdome in 1978; Muhammad Ali fought Leon Spinks.

The biggest crowd for a football game is 121,000 for the then-annual Chicago Mayor's Trophy high school championship in Soldier Field in the 1930s. Notre Dame drew 120,000 to Soldier Field for two games in the 1920s. In baseball, the largest crowd to see a World Series game is 92,706 at Memorial Coliseum in Los Angeles. The Dodgers hosted the Chicago White Sox in 1959.

In basketball, 80,000 fans watched the final of the 1968 European Cup in Athens. For a college basketball game, the record is 66,144 in the Superdome in 1989 to watch Georgetown play Louisiana State. The biggest crowd for a women's college basketball game is 24,563 in Knoxville, Tenn., for Tennessee-Texas in 1987.

In tennis, 30,472 fans in Houston's Astrodome watched an exhibition match between Billy Jean King and Bobby Riggs in 1973, while the biggest crowd for a standard match is 25,578 in Sydney for the 1954 Davis Cup round between Australia and the U.S.

In field hockey, a record 65,165 watched the U.S. and England in London in 1978. In hurling, 84,865 saw the All-Ireland Final in Dublin in 1954. The Jai Alai record is 15,052 fans at the World Jai Alai in Miami in 1975; the capacity of the fronton is only 3,884. And in squash, 3,526 fans attended the 1987 World Team Championships in London.

Meanwhile, among the smallest crowds of all-time: zero, for the Los Angeles Cup '97 soccer doubleheader in the L.A. Coliseum, Jan. 7, 1997. Four professional teams from Mexico and El Salvador played behind closed doors because U.S. soccer officials refused to grant the organizers a permit. And finally, the smallest crowd ever for a heavyweight title fight is 2,434 for the Cassius Clay vs. Sonny Liston rematch in Lewiston, Maine, May 25, 1965.

Restless Fans

Boxing fans got out of hand July 11, 1996, at New York's Madison Square Garden. Riddick Bowe was facing Andrew Golota. After Golota was disqualified for his fifth low blow, a riot erupted. Members of Bowe's entourage went after Golota, who got hit in the head with a walkie-talkie. Golota's 74-year-old trainer, Lou Duva, had to carried out of the arena on a stretcher. Fans began fighting and tossing chairs in the stands. A man was knocked out of his wheelchair. It took police and security officials more than 30 minutes to calm the crowd. In the end, three Bowe camp members were arrested for assault and inciting to riot. A total of 14 fans were arrested. Eight policemen and 14 fans suffered injuries.

That wasn't the first brawl involving boxing fans. In 1980 in London, Marvin Hagler KO'd England's Alan Minter in the third round. But before Hagler could get out of the ring, he was pelted with beer bottles. Security officials tried to escort Hagler to the dressing rooms, but a mob blocked the exit. Finally, Hagler was taken to the security office where officers kept the crowd at bay.

 Boxing fans are not alone. Fans have caused turmoil at every type of sporting event...

- Rugby was dropped as an Olympic sport following the 1924 Games in Paris after rival fans rioted.
- In cricket, fans in Calcutta, upset with the play of the Indian national team, threw rocks and bottles onto the field and set fires in the grandstand at a 1996 match. The referee called off the game, the first forfeit in World Cup history. Pakistani fans weren't too pleased with their team's loss, either. A mob of fans at the airport in Lahore forced the team to divert its flight to another city. The captain of the team, who missed the final match because of an injury, was burned in effigy and received death threats. He was also sued. Later, at the Titan Cup in Bangalore, India, fans protesting a call forced a 20-minute halt in play when they littered the field with plastic bottles, food

and other garbage. And in Peshawar, Pakistan, police had to use batons to control 35,000 spectators who threw stones, bottles and fruit. Fans broke down an iron gate and forced their way into the press box and destroyed the area. Play was halted for a total of 81 minutes.

- At the 1975 Tour de France, a fan determined the outcome. Belgian Eddie Merckx had won five of the six previous races and was ahead again. But a French fan didn't want to see another Tour title leave the country. The fan ran onto the road and punched Merckx, knocking him off his bike. Merckx withdrew from the race the next day because of kidney pain from the attack. The eventual winner was a Frenchman, Bernard Thevenet. The fan was charged with aggravated assault, but was considered a hero by many of his countrymen. One publication called it a crime de passion. "I was overwhelmed by something bigger than me," said the fan.

- Five minutes before the start of the 1986 Winston 500 NASCAR race in Talladega, Ala., fan Darren Crowder hopped into the empty Pontiac Trans-Am pace car sitting in front of the grandstands. Unbelievably, the keys were in the ignition. Crowder started the car and raced onto the track, reaching speeds in excess of 100 m.p.h. Security officials formed a blockade of maintenance trucks at the fourth turn while the police with flashing lights and sirens gave chase. Crowder surrendered and was arrested.

- Russell Howard Caputo ran across the Del Mar race track in San Diego in 1995, narrowly missing the horses driving for the finish line. The 38-year-old man, carrying a duffel bag, jumped the outer rail and began running toward the finish line. The winner, Sea Of Serenity, avoided the man without incident, but the trailing horses missed the man and his duffel bag by mere inches. The man jumped the inner rail, ran across the turf track and was caught near the tote board by a member of the track crew. Caputo, who later made references to suicide, was taken to the County Mental Health treatment facility.

- Fans prevented pole vaulter John Uelses from being credited with breaking a world record. Uelses became the first man to clear 16-feet in 1962 at a meet in New York's Madison Square Garden. But when fans began celebrating near the pit, the cross bar fell off before the height could be measured officially. The record was disallowed. But the story did have a happy ending. The next day in Boston, with officials keeping the fans in the stands, Uelses set the world record by clearing 16' 3/4".

• Harry Veltman III of Riverside, Calif., was arrested for harassment in 1991 for throwing packets of sexually threatening letters at figure skater Katarina Witt. The Olympic skater was performing at Denver's McNichols Sports Arena. Police said the typed letters included sexual threats and indicated "what he wanted to do to her."

• Fans at the 1996 Davis Cup competition in Sao Paolo, Brazil, caused Austrian Thomas Muster to withdraw in the middle of a match. Muster claimed the spectators spat at him, threw objects and tried to blind him with mirrors. He described the fans as "animals."

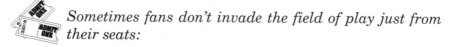 *Sometimes fans don't invade the field of play just from their seats:*

• During Game 2 of the 1919 World Series in Cincinnati, a passenger plane soared over the top of the stadium. When it came closer, play was stopped. As it passed dangerously low over the infield, a human figure flew out the door, fell to the ground and nearly hit the shortstop. A policeman rushed to the "victim." It was only a dummy, and the lawman returned to foul territory and used the dummy as a seat cushion the rest of the game.

• Just 15 minutes after the Steelers-Colts 1976 NFL playoff game, Donald Kroner crashed his single-engine Piper Cherokee airplane into the upper grandstand of Baltimore's Memorial Stadium. According to one of the witnesses: "He came in first out there between the light towers in right field and buzzed over that end, then zoomed out between the light towers in left field. Then he came in over the far goal posts, but then he stalled and when he gunned the motor, he couldn't get it up

AP/Wide World Photos

Michael Sergio parachutes into Shea Stadium during Game 6 of the 1986 World Series.

over the top rim of the stadium. One of the wing tips hit the orange seats and it spun and stuck there." Kroner, 42, survived the crash; three policemen were injured.

- Michael Sergio, a life-long New York Mets fan, parachuted into Shea Stadium during the first inning of Game 6 of the 1986 World Series. The 35-year-old actor carried a "Let's Go Mets" banner and landed on the infield. He was arrested and detained for three weeks when he refused to release the name of the pilot who was flying the plane. "I saw Game 5 in Boston on TV," said Sergio, "and what did they do, release balloons? C'mon! This is New York! There they do balloons. Here we got a human sacrifice!"

- James Miller, a.k.a. "Fan Man," dropped into the ring of the 1993 Evander Holyfield-Riddick Bowe fight at Caesars Palace in Las Vegas. Miller crashed his motorized paraglider when he tried to land in the outdoor ring during the seventh round and got tangled in the canopy lights. He was injured when he fell in Bowe's corner, then took a beating from Bowe's security staff. Bowe's pregnant wife, Judy, fainted. The commotion caused a 21-minute delay.

- Three Army paratroopers, who planned to deliver the game ball for a 1996 high school football game in Washington, landed at the wrong school. The fans and players at River View High School didn't know what to think as a helicopter hovered over the field and the parachutists descended during the pre-game warm-ups. Five miles away, players and fans from Kennewick and Pasco high schools were craning their necks, looking for the parachutists who were supposed to hit the giant "X" in the middle of the field. The Army blamed the mistake on "a new pilot that lost track of his marker." The jumpers found the right field the following week. Meanwhile, officials at River View were so impressed with the surprise landing that they invited the troopers back to the school's Homecoming game.

- A Spanish tobacco company wanted to entertain 30 clients at the 1992 French motorcycle grand prix. A plane was chartered, and the VIPs were flown to La Castallet. That had been the site of the 1991 race. The '92 race, though, was being run 400 miles away at Magny-Cours.

Showin' Some Skin

Melissa Johnson, 23, was a London student when she got a part-time job on the catering staff that serviced the 1996 Wimbledon tennis tournament. She streaked across Centre Court during the men's final between Richard Krajicek and MaliVai Washington. "I looked over, and I see this streaker," said Washington. "I see this, this...wobbling around. She smiled at me, and I think she was wearing an apron. She lifted it up and was still smiling. I got flustered, then three sets later, I was gone." A London betting agency offered 5:1 odds on a streaker crossing the court during the men's or women's final. The statement from Wimbledon officials was, "Whilst we do not wish to condone the practice, it did at least provide some light amusement for our loyal and patient supporters, who have had a trying time during the recent bad weather."

 Through the years, "streakers" have shown up at a number of sporting events. But even streaks have to share the limelight...

- Edy Williams, wife of pornographic film producer Russ Meyer, streaked the Muhammad Ali-Leon Spinks fight in New Orleans' Superdome in 1978.
- The Furness Rugby Union Club in Great Britain tried a unique way of raising money in 1992. It asked the club's female fans to bid on a chance to shower with its players. As an added attraction, the winning bidder was allowed to take a friend to share the experience.
- Fans who worked at The Top of the Town bordello offered to help the players on a local Australian Rules Football team who had been ordered to abstain from sex with their wives or girlfriends. The Sydney Swans were in training for the league's championship game when the players were offered "freebies to help them keep their routine." The brothel added, "If the players are used to having sex, they will feel neglected. It might affect their performance." The Swans wound up losing the game to the North Melbourne Kangaroos, 131-88.

Mascots

Sometimes teams' biggest fans are their mascots. However, sometimes those mascots go a bit too far:
- Oski, the University of California mascot, was suspended in 1990 by the school after he tossed a two-layer cream cake at visiting fans from Oregon State University.
- Meanwhile, the Oregon State mascot, Benny the Beaver, played by Marri Hollen, was slugged by a 6-foot-6, 320-pound California tackle after she hit him on the head with an inflatable hammer during a 1995 game. Later that season, Benny was punched in the face for no apparent reason by a 6-foot-5, 305-pound lineman from the University of Arizona.
- At the University of Maine, students didn't appreciate a campus cafeteria visit by Bananas the Bear. He was pummeled by a group of students, including a forward on the school's basketball team.
- The Washington Bullets mascot, Hoops I, pounded a 13-year-old fan with a plastic baseball bat.
- Slapshot the Puck, the mascot for the New Jersey Devils, was dismissed after being accused of fondling female fans.

• And finally, senior Sherod Reed is the Delta Devil mascot for Mississippi Valley State. He also is the associate pastor at a local church. "People feel that is a double standard being a minister and portraying a devil at the games," said Reed. "They have to realize that I am in a devil uniform, but the devil is not in me. I am a man based on Christian values. I wonder would it matter if the mascot was a tiger?"

Fans also have become famous for dancing at games. One of the most recognizable is Wilford "Crazy Ray" Jones. He is as much a fixture on the sidelines of Dallas Cowboys games as the Cowboys Cheerleaders. He began dancing at games when the team joined the NFL in 1960. However, during the 1997 off-season, Jones had his right foot amputated because of complications from diabetes. Jones said he'll be back on the field for the '97 season. "I may not be as active, but I'll be out there."

Fans and Losing Streaks

• After 10 consecutive losses in 1976, the Boston Red Sox allowed a "witch" to cast a good spell on their bats. Laurie Cabot, from Salem, Mass., flew to Cleveland to help the Sox get "doubles, doubles for their toil and troubles." Indians' coach Mudcat Grant tried to break the spell by casting his own "Lacoochee whammy." Boston won, 6-4. The next day, the Indians brought in a fairy godmother, actually former ball girl Debbie Berndt dressed in a white gown and white wig. She was no match for the real witch. Again, Boston won.

• After the Baltimore Orioles dropped their 15th straight game at the start of the 1988 season, a local radio station called on The Amazing Kreskin for help. Kreskin asked all the Oriole fans to join him in beaming positive thoughts to the team prior to a game. Baltimore pitcher Mike Morgan didn't get the message and didn't get anyone out; the O's gave up nine runs in the first inning on their way to a 13-1 loss.

• The San Jose State University football team offered a $10,000 reward for helping find a famous sorceress prior to its 1996 season. SJSU sought Josephine Canicatti, who in 1955 gained

162

national attention when she placed a spell on New York Yankees manager Casey Stengel. That fall the Yankees lost the World Series, and Stengel lost $200,000 in a bad real estate deal. The 83-year-old woman was last seen in Hollister, Calif., in 1994.

Fans and Religion

- In 1909, "blue laws" forbade many activities on Sundays. Many professional baseball teams avoided playing on the holy day. However, the Jersey City Skeeters decided to try it. Every spectator that day was given a card as they entered the stadium. It read: Please be quiet and do not cheer. The fans remained quiet for the entire game.

- Robin Bechhofer, a fan at the University of Wisconsin women's basketball exhibition game against Athletes in Action in 1995, wrote to local newspapers to complain about the religious overtones. AIA is a team sponsored by Campus Ministry for Christ that plays college teams throughout the nation. Religious pamphlets were distributed to fans during the second half, and speakers offered religious testimonials after the game. Bechhofer's complaints were picked up by Freedom from Religion, a group that advocates strict separation of church and state. The group called for the dismissal of the UW coach, Jane Albright-Dieterle.

- After the fifth inning of most games in Baltimore's Camden Yards, Orthodox Jews congregate in a small kitchen behind a kosher food concession stand for prayer service. As many as three dozen fans take a 15-minute break from the game to pray. Orthodox Jews have three services a day — morning, afternoon and evening. A typical baseball game ends too late for them to find an evening service. The makeshift service never varies. It includes a basic Hebrew prayer, the Shema Yisroel, and 18 benedictions. The men and teenage boys, some wearing baseball caps and some yarmulkes, thank God for what he has done and for his guidance from above.

Controversial Fans

- Edgar Heap of Birds, an associate professor of art at the University of Oklahoma, designed a 25-by-12 foot billboard to be displayed in Cleveland. It featured a drawing of the Cleveland Indians' mascot, Chief Wahoo, and the words, "Smile for Racism." The billboard was supposed to be part of a 1996 exhibition at the Cleveland Institute of Art, but officials at the Institute decided not to put up the billboard.

- Gay baseball fans in San Francisco criticized Giants pitcher Mark Dewey who refused to join in a pregame show of solidarity with AIDS volunteers. Dewey, a fundamentalist Christian, wore a red AIDS ribbon sideways, making the looped ribbon resemble the Christian fish symbol. Jon Pevna, a member of the organizing group, wrote to Giants president Peter Magowan, "Mr. Dewey's behavior...was so repugnant to many of us in the stands that I seriously hope you will consider trading him or giving him his unconditional release."

- U.S. luge athletes were attacked in 1993 in Germany by a group of right-wing skinheads. The luge team, in training at a nearby facility, was celebrating one of the athlete's birthdays at a bar when the skinheads began taunting an African-American luger with Nazi and racist slogans. Another American, Duncan Kennedy, was beaten. Five youths were arrested.

Pretenders

- The most famous impostor of all-time is Barry Bremen. The manufacturer's rep from Birmingham, Mich., appeared as an NBA player at the 1979 All-Star Game, played nine practice holes at the 1979 U.S. Open golf tournament, shagged fly balls in the outfield next to Fred Lynn at the 1981 All-Star Game, and tried to dance with the Dallas Cowboys Cheerleaders. It was that last stunt that got Bremen in the most trouble. The Cowboys hit him with a $5,000 lawsuit for trespassing and creating a nuisance and barred him and his family from Cowboy games for life. "Luckily, I built up a reputation," he said. "As Tommy John told me, I do it in good taste, and I don't disrupt from games that mean something. What I do is All-Star Games, practice rounds, where the players are there on parade, and I do it as a spoof. The only people who don't like it are the executives."

- Rivaling Bremen today is Scott Kerman. The professional comedian and writer doesn't pose as a player, but instead gains entry to big sporting events by posing as a concessionaire or security guard. The 29-year-old from Marina del Rey, Calif., claims to have crashed six Super Bowls, 25 World Series games, and more than 300 sporting events or concerts. He feels no remorse over sneaking in. "Financially, the only money missing from the game is the ticket fee, because you'll still eat hot dogs and drink beer once you enter the event, with or without a ticket. Since you will be occupying an empty seat, you'll actually be upgrading the importance of the event for TV cameras scanning what appears to be a sold-out crowd."

- Rosie Ruiz might be the most infamous impostor. She was the first woman to cross the finish line of the 1980 Boston Marathon. Later it was revealed that she had not run the entire race and her crown was stripped. The 26-year-old New Yorker even had turned in a bogus qualifying time from the New York Marathon. Witnesses claim she completed most of that race on the subway.

- Another marathon impostor was Norbert Sudhous who stole the winning thunder from American Frank Shorter in the 1972 Olympics in Munich. Unbeknownst to Shorter, the impostor entered the stadium a couple of minutes before him and ran a full lap before being discovered. The crowd's cheers turned to jeers, just as Shorter stepped on the track. Shorter was taken aback by the crowd's reaction and didn't know why it had been hostile until after the race.

- Lou Proctor was an impostor who wasn't uncovered for 75 years. For years, Proctor was listed in the *Baseball Encyclopedia* as appearing in one game for the 1912 St. Louis Browns. In 1987, baseball historians found out that Proctor was really a press box telegraph operator who entered his own name in a box score he was transmitting.

- Arthur McDuffy was listed in several college recruiting lists as a top prospect. The 6-foot-6, 300-pounder from Mt. Pleasant (Miss.) Christian Academy could bench press 350 pounds and maintained a 4.0 grade-point average. He was a cinch to land a scholarship to a top school. But when recruiters began calling, they found out that there was no McDuffy and no Mt. Pleasant. The hoax was traced back to the Jackson, Miss., *Clarion-Ledger's* roster of top prospects in the state. An anonymous caller had provided the background on the prospect, and the paper had failed to check the facts.

- But that's nothing compared to a hoax in 1941. Morris Newburger, a partner in a Wall Street brokerage firm, dreamed up an entire football team at a fictitious college. He created "Plainfield Teachers" and came up with a nine-game schedule against other fake schools like Chesterton and Randolph Tech. Then he phoned the *New York Herald-Tribune* every Saturday night with the team's "results." At first, he just called in a score. The next day, it appeared in the newspaper. Then he began adding a few details. He invented a Chinese running back, John Chung, who gained 7.9 yards every time he carried the ball, ate wild rice at halftime and was carried off the field by rickshaw following an injury. He began calling more news outlets and even created a fictitious sports information director to disseminate the news. *The New York Post* received a press release on Chung and wrote an article on him. Plainfield was rolling along with a 7-0 record when Newburger's hoax was tipped to a reporter at the *Herald-Tribune*. Newburger was allowed to write one last press release announcing that poor grades on mid-term examinations had sidelined all but nine players on the team, forcing the school to cancel the remaining games.

The Business of Fans

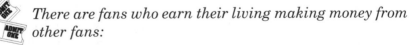 *There are fans who earn their living making money from other fans:*

- Fans who wanted to paint their face or body in the school or team colors used to have to rely on lipstick, eye shadow or grease pencils. But two companies began making special paint for the fans. Buddy Bell, of Lakewood, Ohio, started making Team Colors. He is marketing sticks of zinc oxide, usually at

$4.50 for a pack of three, color-matched to your favorite team. The paint comes in containers resembling lip balm. The colors are unique for every team, so the red for the Washington Redskins is different from the Ohio State Buckeyes. "We used the actual uniforms to choose the colors," Bell said.

Meanwhile, in Bloomfield, N.J., the Klein family came up with GameFace. The Kleins use commercial Halloween makeup applied with a tongue depressor. The brochure marketing GameFace says, "Watching the game should not be a spectator sport."

- If you don't want to take the time to paint your school's logo on your cheek, then consider applying a temporary tattoo. Highgate Products Inc. in Dallas offers the tattoos for $2-$4 each.

- And if a tattoo isn't striking enough, then San Francisco Supercuts Inc. hair care chain is for you. It features cuts that shave team emblems on your head. Sales are reportedly brisk.

- A fan in Troy, N.Y., received a patent to produce a mechanical arm that gives a TV viewer at home a high five.

- Gary Miller and Mark D. Kaplan started Sportsfund, a mutual fund that invested at least 65 percent of the assets in equity securities of public companies that engage in sports-related activities. Investors could get in with a minimum of $1,000. On Nov. 8, 1996, Sportsfund completed its first quarter of operation with a three-month 4.10 percent total return. Among the companies Sportsfund invested in were: Brunswick, Fountain Powerboat, National Golf Properties Inc. and Penn National Gaming.

- Fans who have difficulty paying for their season tickets now have a choice. Many banks offer loans to support the local team. In New Jersey, Constellation Bank had a "bowl-bound" savings account for Rutgers fans to set aside cash for the trip if the school went to a post-season game. Several banks in Charlotte helped Panthers fans pay for permanent seat licenses with low-cost loans. Nearly every team and school has a bank-assisted affinity credit card. Proceeds from card purchases normally go toward paying for scholarships or team foundations.

Other fans prefer trying to make big money off sports by gambling:

- Stephen Conway of Rohnert Park, Calif., won $10.87 million in the California lottery by playing the uniform numbers of his favorite players: Archie Griffin (45), Mickey Mantle (7), Bob Cousy (5), Bill Walton (32), Roberto Clemente (21) and Terry Bradshaw (12). But wait. Didn't Cousy wear No. 14? Yep, but Conway's goof permitted him to win. Sometimes it's better to be lucky than right.
- Anthony A. Speelman and Nicholas John Cowan, both from Great Britain, won $1,627,084.40, after federal income tax of $406,768 was withheld, at Santa Anita (Calif.) Racetrack, Apr. 19, 1987. It was the biggest pay-out ever on a pari-mutuel bet. The pair bet $64 on a nine-horse accumulator. Their first seven picks won, and the pay-out was a jackpot that had accumulated for 24 days.
- A sports fan's dream is to be able to bet on a game that already was played. Such was the case Jan. 2, 1996, in Toronto. Pro-Line, the state-run sports-betting operation, took bets on British soccer games until 2 p.m. (7 p.m. in England), the usual kickoff time for weekday games. However, Jan. 2 was a holiday in Britain, and four of that day's games were played in the afternoon. A group of fans at a Toronto pub realized its opportunity and called Britain to get that day's results. Pro-Line, which honored the winning tickets even after it realized the mistake, paid out about $550,000. That's five times the normal level for the amount wagered. None of the lucky winners has gone public, though, probably to avoid paying taxes.

Big Fans

- Muhammad Ali fan Chris Sininger promised to get Ali's 1960 Olympic gold medal replaced. Ali threw his medal into the Ohio River to protest a racist incident in his hometown of Louisville. It took Sininger four years and help from then-Vice President Dan Quayle to live up to his promise. In Atlanta at the 1996 Olympics, the new medal was awarded to Ali. The replica was made by Huguenin Medailleurs in Switzerland,

168

the firm that makes all the Olympic medals.

- Steve Moore is a sports fan who parlayed his passion into a career. A news editor at the *Los Angeles Times,* Moore developed, then syndicated the comic, *In the Bleachers.* It looks at the world of sports with a touch of humor.
- Another comic artist, Milton A. Caniff, was one of the biggest sports fans at his alma mater, Ohio State University. Caniff was the creator of *Terry and the Pirates* and *Steve Canyon.* As a student at OSU (1926-30), he sat in the Block O cheering section for home football games and drew cover artwork for most of the game programs. He incorporated many of the OSU players and coaches into his comics over the years, until his death in 1987.
- Kevin Quirk admits he was a sportsaholic. Now the 41-year-old from Charlottesville, Va., is writing a book, *Not Now Honey, I'm Watching the Game.* He's trying to make other sportsaholics aware of their addiction. He admits it was a factor in his divorce, and it can rip apart a family.

How Fans Begin and End

A couple of young sports fans fulfilled a fantasy, as well as embarked on a possible career:

- Six-year-old Michael Douglas Fraser of North York, Ontario, was a special play-by-play announcer for FOX's national telecast of the Chicago Cubs-Cincinnati Reds game, June 29, 1996. He won a contest on the network's Internet site. Originally, Fraser was just going to get to observe the action in the broadcast booth, but after producer Michael Weisman met him, the lad was allowed to announce the sixth inning. "Our goal was not to find the next Vin Scully or Mel Allen," Weisman said. "Our goal was to look at the game through the innocent eyes of a 6-year-old, to go back to the time when we were all kids and went to the ballpark for the first time and took in all the sights and sounds."
- Nine-year-old Sparky Mortimer has become somewhat of a regular on *Late Show with David Letterman.* The Utah native has been the show's correspondent for the World Series and Super Bowl after first appearing on the show in September, 1993.

Sometimes the addiction continues even after a fan has died:

- A few days after the New York Yankees won the 1996 World Series, Eddie Ellner was on a plane in California en route to Yankee Stadium. Next to him were the ashes of Betty Fein, his grandmother. Fein was an avid Yankees fan who died in 1990 at the age of 82. Her dying wish was that if the Yankees ever won another World Series, she wanted her ashes scattered across the field. Ellner spread the ashes on home plate, the on-deck circle, along the first base line and over the infield.

- In Chicago, the dying wish of a Cubs fan was honored during the seventh-inning stretch of a 1996 game when the deceased's son reached over the Wrigley Field bleacher railing and gently shook his father's ashes onto the warning track and into the vines that cover the brick wall. "(The son) was asked to leave the park (after scattering the ashes), which he did, because he had accomplished what he came to do," said Mike Hill, manager of event operations at Wrigley.

- Horse racing handicapper Leo Underhill was at New York's Saratoga Racetrack nearly every day. When he died in 1996, the track honored Underhill's request to have his ashes buried at the finish line.

- At Buffalo's Rich Stadium, a group of "fans" never makes any noise. Outside Gate 7 stands the Sheldon Family Cemetery. The Sheldons began burying their dead in the plot in the 1830s. There are about a dozen marked sites and an undetermined number of unmarked graves. The last person buried there was in the 1940s. When the Stadium was built in the 1970s, the burial grounds were not disturbed. It was preserved and today sits surrounded by a fence and a flurry of activity 10 times a year.

- Giants Stadium might also be the site of a grave. Donald "Tony the Greek" Frankos, a federally protected mob witness, said former Teamster boss Jimmy Hoffa was shot to death by mob-hired hitmen near Detroit in July, 1975. He said the body was cut into pieces and stored in a freezer for five months before being packed into an oil drum, trucked to the Meadowlands and dumped in Giants Stadium, which was under construction at the time.

- Syracuse University football, basketball and lacrosse fans parked along the lanes of Oakwood Cemetery near the Carrier Dome for the past 20 years. But families who own plots in the cemetery complained that garbage — including empty beer cans — was left on the stately grounds. So, fans no longer are permitted to use the area as a parking lot.
- Former Houston Oilers coach Jerry Glanville used to leave free tickets at the Will Call Window for a number of dead fans. For a 1988 preseason game in Memphis, he left tickets for Elvis Presley; Hoosier-born actor James Dean was a no-show for the Oilers-Colts game in Indianapolis; Buddy Holly didn't collect his free tickets at the box office for a game in Dallas; and for an Oilers-Jets game in New York, a sideline pass went unused for the Phantom of the Opera.
- Frank Pew attended every Canadian Football League home game of the British Columbia Lions for nearly 40 years. He died at the age of 94. To honor Pew, the team kept his seat — Section 42, Row BB, Seat 3 — empty.
- Philadelphia Eagles wide receiver Irving Fryar moved into 11th place on the NFL's all-time receiving list during the 1996 season. He became a fan favorite. "A young lady came to our facility the other day and asked me to sign a jersey," Fryar said. "She said one of her family members had passed away and wanted to be buried in my jersey. Knowing somebody thinks that much of me, and wanted to be buried in my jersey, I've just got to play hard."

Sports Trivia

A lot of fans are entertained and fascinated by sports trivia. It's not enough to know who the only player killed in a Major League Baseball game was (Ray Chapman). You also need to know who the pitcher was (Carl Mays), as well as the pinch runner (Harry Lunte).

- There are 800 members in the North American Society for Sport History, founded in 1974. It publishes a triannual *Jour-*

nal of Sport History, sends out newsletters and announcements about research projects and hosts an annual convention.

- In Minneapolis, radio station WCCO has conducted Minnesota Sports Trivia Bowls. In 1984, their first year, there were 200 four-person teams. One of the questions that stumped both teams in the finals: According to the poem "Casey at the Bat," what was the attendance in Mudville when Casey struck out? (The answer: 5,000.)

- Floyd Satterlee Rodd didn't know he'd someday be the answer to the trivia question, "Who played a golf course that was 5,980,480 yards long?" That's exactly what Rodd did in 1963-64 when he hit golf balls from the Pacific surf to the Atlantic Ocean. He covered the 3,398 miles in 114,737 strokes and lost 3,511 balls. (No report, though, of whether he took a stroke and distance penalty for each lost ball.)

Hitting the Links

- Jamie Hutton, a 17-year-old from Madison, Wis., walked alongside Greg Norman as the Australian golfer won the 1988 Heritage Classic on Hilton Head Island. Hutton was given the trip by Thursday's Child, which attempts to grant the wishes of seriously ill young people. Hutton had leukemia. Norman gave Hutton the winner's jacket and trophy. "He showed me inspiration and courage," said Norman. "He told me he wanted me to shoot 64 and win. I shot a 66 and that was enough."

- Bruce Charles, a six-handicapper from West Peabody, Mass., was watching Greg Norman in a practice round prior to the 1988 U.S. Open. In the rough off the 14th green, Norman hit a wedge about 20 feet from the hole. Charles hollered, "That shot wasn't so hard." Norman replied, "Come out here, expert." Charles took Norman's wedge and put the ball within five feet of the cup. Norman gave Charles a high five and the ball.

- Norman wasn't as kind to another heckler at the 1996 MCI Classic at Hilton Head. Norman was on the 18th tee in the third round when a fan called Norman a "choker" and said the golfer had cost him a lot of money. Norman asked the fan if he had a problem, and Norman's caddie, Tony Navarro, charged the fan and knocked him to the ground. The fan, whose name was not released by tournament officials, was ejected and arrested.

- Talia Bennett, an 18-year-old at Marcos DeNiza High School in Tempe, Ariz., was one of 18 young golfers who got to participate in Dream Day '97. The students got to play a three-hole exhibition match with pros Tiger Woods, Phil Mickelson and Billy Mayfair prior to the 1997 Phoenix Open. Bennett's experience was especially rewarding. She tied Woods on the 300-yard 10th hole with a par-4. "He's just a normal person," Bennett said about Woods. "He talked about being so hungry. He said, 'I want a Whopper.'"

- Laura Davies had a problem with an obsessed fan on the LPGA Tour. A retired surgeon from Canada followed her for three years, asking her to marry him. He showed up at the 1995 U.S. Women's Open with a copy of his divorce papers. "He's a fruitcake," said Davies. "I hope he's harmless, but you never know about people with obsessions."

- Chuck MacDonald of Willis, Mich., was sitting on a folding stool near the 16th green, watching the second round of the 1996 U.S. Open. First, Steve Lowery's approach shot bounced off the right side of MacDonald's forehead. Then a ball hit by Payne Stewart smacked MacDonald on the top of his head, causing a four-inch gash. As MacDonald was escorted to a first-aid station, Stewart gave him the ball and a glove. "Send me the check if you win," MacDonald said.

- A trash container near the first tee exploded at the 1996 World Series of Golf in Akron. Vicky Miller of Fairlawn Heights, Ohio, had her chest bruised when she was hit by an unidentified object. Two other fans were treated for minor injuries. "It was some type of a homemade fireworks device. It was definitely not a pipe bomb, but something along the lines of an M-100 or something larger," said Terry Livers, a tournament official.

We've All Been There

And finally, no matter what the sport, the site or the level of play, there's one part of being a fan that no one can ignore: restrooms.

- Architects revealed that when the Arizona Diamondbacks' new Bank One Ballpark opens in 1998, women's toilets will out-number men's, 340-55. "We've been assured that the capacity is going to be a happy situation," said John Wasson, the project manager.

- That decision may have stemmed from a near brawl in St. Louis' Busch Memorial Stadium in 1986. The female fans at the Car-dinals-Cubs game grew tired of standing in lines to use the restrooms. Scores of women stormed the men's rooms. Said one disgruntled male fan, "I offered to share my urinal with one of the gals, but she told me to buzz off. I was just trying to be hospitable. After all, this was a men's john."

- Marie Higgins is doing her part to assure a new stadium in Detroit provides enough restrooms for the female fans. "Men have it so easy," she told *The Detroit News*. "They get in and get out in a few seconds. Women are just as big of sports fans as men and have it a lot harder. Architects putting up the new stadiums should remember that." Studies show that women spend about twice as long to use the restroom as men.

- Fans at the 1996 Summer Olympics in Atlanta were just as concerned. Guidelines showed that the crowd of 600,000 needed 3,300 Port-O-Lets. However, the organizing committee rented just 2,000 portable toilets. City officials asked the downtown restaurants, hotels and retailers to open their hearts and stalls.

- Raiders fans were asked in 1996 not to use the Oakland Coli-seum restrooms after halftime. The flushing of the toilets caused the water pressure in the players' dressing rooms to drop to a level that made it impossible to use the showers.

- Sick's Stadium in Seattle was undergoing some reconstruction in 1969, so portable toilets were placed in the bleacher areas for fans of the Seattle Pilots. A fan got trapped in a temporary john and was forced to spend the night in it. A member of the clean-up crew heard him screaming the next morning. "They unlocked the door, and he took off on a dead run," said Bill Sears, a club spokesman. "We never did find out who he was. God only knows what kind of an excuse he gave his wife when he got home."

ABOUT THE
AUTHORS

Rich Wolfe

Rich Wolfe is a native of Lost Nation, Ia. (A one-horse town. He wanted to leave when he was 15, but the horse was sick.)

He played basketball and baseball at the University of Notre Dame and graduated in 1965. As a sports fan he's run the gamut from being in the Mets' locker room when they won the 1969 World Series to being the only person to walk off Tom Watson's famous chip shot that won the 1982 U.S. Open. (It was 16-and-a-half feet.)

Wolfe is a long-time marketing consultant to major and minor league sports franchises and currently owns teams in the Central Hockey League.

Dale Ratermann

Dale Ratermann is a native of Marion, Ill. He graduated from the University of Illinois in 1978.

His first experience as a fan at a major sporting event was Stan Musial's final game in St. Louis in 1963 (at age 7). His most recent experience was at the 1996 National Finals Rodeo. In between, he has witnessed — usually from the cheap seats — nearly every type of sporting event.

He has written several books.

DO YOU HAVE A GOOD FAN STORY?

A message to the readers, from Rich and Dale:

Do you know someone who would make a good addition to this book? Then tell us. We're already planning for *More Sports Fans Who Made Headlines*. (Publisher's Note: Hey, wait a minute! We'd love to have a second edition of *Sports Fans*, but not unless this first edition sells enough copies to warrant a second one. So, if you want to see you or your friends included in the next book, go out and buy 17 more copies of this one. Or better yet, make a list and send a book to each person on the list and instruct that person to add to that list and send a book to everyone on their list and pretty soon you'll have 50,000 copies of this book that you can unload at a used book store for lots of money and rest in the satisfaction that you helped create the best-selling sports book of all-time.)

As we were saying, we're already working on the Second Edition. Send your favorite story, along with a newspaper clipping or other documentation to:

> *Sports Fans Who Made Headlines*
> c/o Masters Press
> Suite 100
> 2647 Waterfront Parkway East Drive
> Indianapolis, IN 46214

The first person to submit each anecdote used will be given credit. Thanks.